STOP PLAYING
S M A L L

GO PUBLIC
BUILD AN
EMPIRE

You're Not 'Too Small' for an IPO.
You're Just Thinking Too Small.
Let's Change That…

STOP PLAYING SMALL

GO PUBLIC BUILD AN EMPIRE

You're Not 'Too Small' for an IPO.
You're Just Thinking Too Small.
Let's Change That…

CA DR. SUNIL GUPTA

SME IPO Speaker, Advisor, and Anchor Investor

Worldwide Published by
Pendown Press

PENDOWN PRESS LLP
An ISO 9001 & ISO 14001 Certified Co.,
Regd. Office: 3767A, Kanhaiya Nagar,
Tri Nagar, Delhi-110035
Ph.: 8130886000, 9650072927
E-mail: info@pendownpress.com
Branch Office: 1A/2A, 20, Hari Sadan, Ansari Road,
Daryaganj, New Delhi-110002
Ph.: 011-45794768
Website: PendownPress.com

Edition: 2025

ISBN: 978-93-6338-422-4

Layout and Cover Designed by Pendown Graphics Team
Printed and Bound in India by Thomson Press India Ltd.

To the Silent Strength Behind My Success

To my **parents, Late Smt. Kusum Gupta and Shri Chetan Gupta**, my first mentors—the ones who taught me the true meaning of hard work, discipline, and resilience. Your unwavering belief in my potential and the quiet sacrifices you made have **shaped the foundation of my journey.** Every lesson you instilled in me continues to guide my path, and for that, **I am eternally grateful.**

And to my wife, Mrs. Sujata Gupta, my partner in every sense—thank you for being my pillar of strength, my sounding board, and my greatest supporter. Your patience, encouragement, and unwavering faith in my vision have fueled my ambition and given me the courage to push forward, even in the toughest moments. This journey would not have been the same without you by my side.

This book is not just a product of my knowledge and experiences but also a **reflection of the love, sacrifices, and support** that you all have given me. I dedicate this work to you, with **deep gratitude and endless appreciation.**

TABLE OF CONTENTS

Going public is just the beginning. Now, let's explore how it changes the game forever.

PART 6: FINAL WORDS – MAKING YOUR MOVE   141

You've Seen the Blueprint. Now It's Time to Execute.

Chapter 20:
The Biggest Regret of Most Business Owners –   **145**
Waiting Too Long

BONUS CHAPTER

Resources to Continue Your Business Growth Journey

MASTER CHECKLIST

Acknowledgments

Writing this book has been a journey of deep exploration, relentless effort, and a shared vision to empower SMEs with the knowledge and tools they need to take their businesses to the next level. But no great work is ever accomplished alone.

I would like to extend my deepest gratitude to my incredible team, the backbone of this mission. Your dedication, expertise, and commitment to supporting businesses in their IPO journey have been instrumental in shaping not just this book, but the very impact we create every day.

A special thanks to **CA Iti Jain, Mohit Jindal, and Supratibh Jain**—your insights, research, and unwavering support have played a crucial role in bringing this book to life. From refining complex concepts to ensuring accuracy and depth in every chapter, your contributions have been invaluable.

This book is a reflection of the collective knowledge, experience, and passion that we, as a team, bring to the table. It is a product of our shared commitment to **helping business owners unlock their full potential and seize the opportunities that lie ahead.**

To everyone who played a part in this journey—thank you. Your belief in this vision has made all the difference.

– CA Dr. Sunil Gupta

SME IPO Speaker, Advisor, and Anchor Investor

FOREWORD

WAKE UP! YOU'RE SITTING ON A GOLDMINE

By CA (Dr.) Sunil Gupta & Industry Expert

Stop. Take a good, hard look at your business. What do you see?

Some clients? A handful of decent sales? Maybe a couple of solid years of "stable" profits? Sounds nice... if your goal is to stay small forever. But if there's even a **spark of ambition** in you—if you've ever caught yourself wondering, **"What if this could be bigger?"**—then what you're doing right now isn't growth. It's survival. And survival mode is a **death sentence** for any business with real potential.

Let me give it to you straight: **You're sitting on a goldmine, and you're too busy running in circles to notice.**

See, small business owners love to talk about "expansion" and "next-level growth." Yet, when it comes to actually **making it big**, they freeze. Why? Because deep down, there's this nagging voice whispering, **"But my business isn't scalable... I'm not that big... Going public is for the Tatas and Reliances of the world, not for someone like me."**

That voice? **It's lying to you.**

Your business isn't small because of its size—
it's small because of the way you think.

THE KALPVRIKSHA: UNLIMITED GROWTH FOR THOSE WHO DARE

Now, let me hit you with a story.

In ancient Hindu mythology, there's the **Kalpvriksha**—a **wish-fulfilling tree** that grants whatever you desire. **Wealth. Growth. Success.** Whatever you ask for, the tree delivers—**no strings attached.**

Sounds like a fairy tale, right? But here's the real twist:

That **same kind of unlimited potential** exists in your business **right now.**

You just can't see it because you've been **stuck in your comfort zone.**

> *"Success comes not from staying where you are, but from having the courage to take the road less traveled."*
> — *Narayan Murthy*

Here's what most small business owners don't get:

Growth doesn't come from **clinging to control** or **saving every rupee** like it's your lifeline. It comes from **tapping into bigger, smarter money.**

And guess what?

An IPO is exactly that. It's your **Kalpvriksha.**

Real Stories: Ordinary Businesses, Extraordinary Growth

You think **only billion-dollar giants** can go public? **Wrong.**

SMEs across India are cracking the **IPO code**—and they're doing it with **turnovers you wouldn't believe.**

Let's break that down:

- **Avax Apparels & Ornaments Ltd** went public with an IPO of just **₹1.92 crore.**

- **Hamps Bio Ltd (previously HEMP Bio)** had a turnover of just **₹6.5 crore** and a profit of ₹50 lakh. They raised ₹6 crore through their IPO.

- **Total SME IPO listings till December 2024:** *Over 1000*

- **Total capital raised through SME IPOs:** *More than ₹20,000 crores*

- **SME Market Capitalization as of Dec 2024:** *₹2.8 lakh crore*

And these aren't **exceptions.** These are businesses **just like yours.**

No boardrooms **full of Harvard grads.** No billion-rupee **R&D budgets.** No **international investors.**

Just **regular business owners** who got **tired of playing small** and **made the bold move to go public.**

The Hidden Cost of Staying Private

So here's the **brutal truth:**

Staying private **isn't protecting your business. It's suffocating it.**

Every year, thousands of small businesses **grind it out**—stuck in a loop of:

√   Limited capital

√   High-interest loans

√   Slow growth

Meanwhile, the **big players**—Reliance, Infosys, Zomato—are **raising capital, expanding, and dominating.**

But here's what **no one tells you**:

They **weren't giants** when they started. **They became giants BECAUSE they went public.**

Now, let me show you the **real risk**—the cost of **staying small.**

That **business idea** you keep saying has **massive potential**? Someone else **is going to steal it.**

Not because they're **smarter.** Not because they're **more innovative.** Not because they're **better than you.**

But because they had the **guts to go public,** raise capital, and **scale faster than you.**

What If Your Competitor Goes Public Before You?

Think about it.

- You stay private, **struggling for capital.**
- Your competitor **gets an IPO,** raises ₹50 crore, and **expands aggressively.**
- Suddenly, they have **better branding, better hiring, and better investors.**
- **You're out of the game.**

And here's the **worst part**—they might not even be **as good as you.**

They just **understood the power of going public** before you did.

The Business Growth Cheat Code: IPO Funding

IPO funding **isn't about losing control**.

It's about **gaining momentum**.

It's about **using other people's money** to build **your empire**.

Let me give you a **real example**.

V-Guard Industries

In 1977, **Kochouseph Chittilappilly** founded a small voltage stabilizer manufacturing unit in Kochi, Kerala, with an initial capital of ₹100,000 and just two employees.

Over the years, V-Guard diversified its product range to include electrical cables, pumps, motors, geysers, and more. The company went public in 2008, listing on both the NSE and BSE. This move provided the necessary capital to expand its operations, leading to a significant increase in revenue and market presence across India.

This transformation from a modest manufacturing unit to a publicly listed company exemplifies how strategic decisions, like launching an IPO, can drive substantial business growth and expansion.

This Book Will Give You the Playbook

In these pages, we **won't** bore you with corporate jargon. This is **real talk, real strategies, real case studies.**

We'll break down:

√ **The hidden mechanics of IPO success** that 90% of businesses miss.

√ **The myths about losing control**—and why they're dead wrong.

√ **The step-by-step process** to take your company public, raise millions, and **still be the boss.**

√ **How small Indian companies** went public and **won big.**

This isn't just another business book.

This is your **growth accelerator**—your **sword, your Sudharshan Chakra, your business steroid.**

This Book Is Your Wake-Up Call

If you're looking for **comfortable** strategies, **close this book now.**

If you want to keep believing that **your business is "too small" or "too risky"** for an IPO—**walk away.**

But **know this:**

While **you hesitate**, someone else is **taking action.**

While **you make excuses**, someone else is **listing shares.**

While **you cling to the "small business" mindset**, someone else is **using public capital to scale and leave you behind.**

So, which one are you?

The **next move** is **on you.**

Turn the page and take control.

Or **close this book and stay exactly where you are.**

Your **call.**

The **Kalpvriksha** is right in front of you.

All you have to do… **is plant the seed.**

DISCLAIMER

General Information Only: This book is intended for informational and educational purposes only. It is not intended to provide, and should not be construed as, financial, legal, investment, or business advice. The information contained herein is based on publicly available sources, industry insights, and the author's professional experience; however, it should not be considered a substitute for consulting with a qualified financial, legal, or investment professional.

No Guarantees or Warranties: While every effort has been made to ensure the accuracy and reliability of the information presented in this book, the author and publisher make no representations or warranties, express or implied, regarding the completeness, accuracy, timeliness, or reliability of the content. Business decisions, particularly those related to IPOs, financial investments, and corporate structuring, carry inherent risks. The author and publisher assume no liability for any losses or damages incurred as a result of the information provided.

No Investment or Legal Advice: Nothing in this book constitutes professional financial, legal, or investment advice. Readers should seek independent professional guidance before making any financial or business decisions, especially regarding IPOs, funding, and public listings. The author and publisher do not hold any responsibility for the financial success or failure of any decisions made based on the contents of this book.

Third-Party References & Trademarks: This book references certain companies, case studies, and real-world examples for educational purposes. All trademarks, registered trademarks, and brand names mentioned belong to their respective owners.

The use of these names does not imply any affiliation with or endorsement by these entities. Any claims, data, or insights are based on publicly available information and should not be considered direct statements from these organizations.

SEBI & Financial Regulations: This book does not serve as an official guide or directive for investment practices under any financial regulatory authority, including the Securities and Exchange Board of India (SEBI). Any references to IPO strategies, funding mechanisms, or valuation tactics are intended for informational purposes only and do not constitute legal or regulatory advice.

Forward-Looking Statements: Some discussions in this book may include forward-looking statements about financial markets, IPO performance, or investment outcomes. These statements are speculative in nature and are subject to risks and uncertainties. Past performance of companies or market trends does not guarantee future results.

Reader Responsibility: The reader acknowledges that they are responsible for their own decisions and due diligence. The author and publisher are not responsible for any direct, indirect, incidental, or consequential damages resulting from the use of information in this book.

By reading this book, you acknowledge and agree to this disclaimer in full.

About the Author

CA Dr. Sunil Gupta is a **seasoned SME IPO Advisor, Chartered Accountant, and financial strategist** with over **22 years of experience** in business consulting, capital markets, and regulatory compliance. Having worked extensively with **businesses ranging from ₹10 Cr to ₹2,000 Cr turnover,** he has been at the forefront of guiding enterprises through the complex journey of **public listing and financial growth.**

Dr. Gupta is the **Founder and Managing Partner of G Sunil & Associates,** where he has helped transform businesses through strategic IPO planning, compliance, and capital fundraising. His expertise lies in **end-to-end IPO advisory,** covering everything from **initial assessment to market debut and post-IPO financial structuring.**

A Legacy of Impact & Expertise

Dr. Gupta's deep industry insights and hands-on experience have led him to:

→ **Coach 1,000+ Chartered Accountants** on SME IPO strategies and financial best practices

→ Conduct **12,000+ hours of 1-on-1 consultations** with business owners across industries

→ **10000+ IPO Related** Questions Answered for Business Owners.

→ Personally **answer 600+ IPO-related questions**, addressing real concerns from SME owners

→ Serve as a **Guest Speaker & Special Invitee** at prestigious financial and business events, including ICAI, ICSI, capital market discussions, MSME government seminars, and various renowned business organizations.

An Authority in SME IPOs & Capital Markets

Dr. Gupta is a recognized expert in financial planning and regulatory compliance, serving on the **Capital Market Committee on Financial Markets and Investors' Protection, NIRC of ICAI**. His insights have played a crucial role in helping SMEs navigate market trends, optimize valuation, and attract investors.

He is also associated with a SEBI-registered Category III, open-ended Alternative Investment Fund (AIF), focused on deploying advanced strategies to deliver strong returns in dynamic market conditions—giving investors and businesses access to innovative funding and wealth creation opportunities.

Through his firm, he has successfully helped multiple companies get listed on the **NSE SME and BSE SME exchanges,** with many of these IPOs achieving remarkable growth post-listing. His work extends beyond IPOs, offering businesses **strategic financial restructuring, fundraising support, and investment planning.**

A Mission to Empower Businesses

Dr. Sunil Gupta's core mission is to **educate and empower SMEs** with the knowledge and tools they need to **scale, attract investors, and build legacy businesses.** He believes that every business is sitting on **a goldmine of opportunities**—and with the right guidance, they can **unlock their full potential through an IPO.**

Beyond his professional pursuits, **Dr. Gupta is also the Founder of SampoornMe,** a health-focused NGO working to spread physical and mental well-being across society. Through free sessions on yoga, fitness, stress management, and wellness, SampoornMe empowers individuals and families to lead healthier, happier lives—one habit at a time.

This book is a **culmination of his decades of experience**, bringing together **battle-tested strategies, real-life case studies, and actionable insights** to help business owners master the **SME IPO journey in India.**

If you're serious about scaling your business and **unlocking the wealth hidden within it,** this book will be your ultimate roadmap.

WHY READ THIS BOOK?

Going for an **SME IPO** is one of the biggest moves a business owner can make—but most don't even know **where to start** or **who to trust** for the right guidance.

That's where this book comes in.

CA Dr. Sunil Gupta has spent **decades in the trenches** helping businesses navigate the complex world of IPOs. His numbers speak for themselves:

- 1,000+ Chartered Accountants Coached
- 12,000+ Hours of 1-on-1 Business Consultations
- Worked with Businesses from ₹10 Cr to ₹2,000 Cr Turnover
- 1,000+ Business Owners Transformed
- 10,000+ IPO Related Questions Answered for Business Owners

Through **years of hands-on experience,** countless deep-dive discussions with business owners, and guiding companies of all sizes through the IPO journey, CA Dr. Sunil Gupta has gathered a **wealth of knowledge**—and now, he's **condensed it all into this book.**

Consider this your Bible for SME IPOs in India. Everything you need to know—**from valuation to investor attraction, regulatory must-knows to execution strategies**—is laid out in **clear, practical steps.**

If you're serious about taking your business public and unlocking the next level of **growth, credibility, and wealth**, this book is your roadmap.

Are you ready to dig into your **goldmine?**

THE BLIND MAN, THE MISSED GOLD, AND THE WINDOW OF OPPORTUNITY

Every successful person—whether in **business, life, or investing**—has one thing in common: they **recognize opportunity when it knocks.**

The problem? **Most people don't.**

They either **fail to see it, hesitate too long, or convince themselves it's not meant for them**. And when they finally realize what they've lost, it's too late—the **window has closed.**

Opportunities don't come with a **neon sign flashing, "Take me!"** They come disguised as **challenges, risks, or decisions that require courage.**

Robin Sharma, in The Greatness Guide, calls these "windows of opportunity"—and how you respond to them defines your destiny. That idea stuck with me, because it's real.

In those moments, you have two choices:

- **Step forward, take the risk, and grab what's yours.**
- **Or hesitate, walk past it, and spend the rest of your life wondering, "What if?"**

To help you truly understand this, here are **two stories**—one from **ancient wisdom** and one from the **modern business world**. Both share the same truth:

Those who fail to recognize opportunity always lose.

The Blind Man Who Missed His Gold

There was once a poor man who had nothing—**no food, no clothes, and no certainty about his future.** But there was one thing he did without fail: **he worshipped Lord Shiva every day, trusting that one day, his prayers would be answered.**

One day, as **Lord Shiva and Goddess Parvati** were passing through his village, Parvati noticed the poor man and said,

"This man is your devotee. He prays to you daily. Can't you bless him with wealth and prosperity?"

Lord Shiva replied,

"I could, but blessings alone won't change his life. He does not know how to **recognize opportunities** when they come his way. If a person cannot see the opportunities around him, no matter how much fortune comes his way, he will still remain where he is."

Goddess Parvati, moved by compassion, insisted that the man deserved a chance. So, to test him, **Lord Shiva scattered gold coins** along the path the poor man was about to walk.

"Now let's see what happens," Shiva said.

As the poor man walked down the road, he thought to himself,

"I am already struggling. I barely have clothes to wear, and soon, I will lose my eyesight. How will I survive if I become blind?"

And so, **to prepare for blindness, he closed his eyes** and started walking with his arms stretched forward, **never once opening them** to see what was in front of him.

Unknowingly, he walked right past the gold coins that had been placed in his path. When he reached the other side, he opened his eyes and thanked God for guiding him safely. He never realized that he had just stepped over the very wealth he had been praying for his whole life.

Goddess Parvati was stunned.

"What just happened? You gave him his chance, and he still walked away with nothing!"

Lord Shiva sighed and said,

"This is what happens when people refuse to see the opportunities around them. They walk through life **blind to the chances that could change everything.** If he had only opened his eyes, he would have seen the fortune that lay right in front of him. The truth is, **a person's destiny is not written in stone—it is created by the decisions they make."**

The Business Owner Who Watched Others Win

This story repeats itself **every single day in business.**

Imagine a business owner who has been working for years. He has built something from the ground up, poured everything into his work, and sacrificed time, money, and effort. But despite his struggles, he is stuck.

He watches **competitors raise funding, expand their brands, and turn their companies into industry leaders.** He **wonders why he's still struggling while others move ahead.**

One day, an advisor tells him about an **SME IPO**—an opportunity to **go public, attract investors, and take his business to the next level.**

But instead of seizing it, **he hesitates.**

"I'm not ready."

"Maybe next year."

"What if something goes wrong?"

So, **he does nothing.**

Months later, he sees another business—one that was **much smaller than his**—go public and grow exponentially. He watches them **raise funding, get featured in news articles, and dominate the market.**

And that's when it hits him.

That could have been me.

But by the time he realizes it, the window has closed.

The Lesson: Opportunities Don't Wait

Whether it's the **poor man walking past gold** or the **business owner ignoring an IPO opportunity,** the lesson is the same.

Fortune favors those who recognize and seize their chances.

Those who hesitate get left behind.

Opportunities don't come every day, and when they do, they don't wait.

Right now, **you are standing at your own window of opportunity.**

Your business has the **potential to grow, expand, and attract serious investment—**but **only if you open your eyes and take action.**

This book will show you e**xactly how to do that.** It is a **step-by-step roadmap** to help you **see what's possible, understand the SME IPO process, and grab the opportunity before it slips away.**

The gold is in front of you. The question is: Will you open your eyes and take it?

ON STAGE & BEYOND: SPREADING FINANCIAL WISDOM ACROSS INDIA

Over the past two decades, I've had the privilege of sharing insights on SME IPOs, financial planning, and business growth at numerous prestigious forums, seminars, and workshops across India.

These events have allowed me to connect with thousands of business owners, Chartered Accountants, and financial professionals, contributing to a growing ecosystem of knowledge and opportunity.

Here are some moments from my journey—capturing the mission to empower, educate, and inspire.

Kratrthata 2025 – 73rd Annual Award Function, NIRC of ICAI

Delivered a high-impact keynote on **"Beyond Compliance: Chartered Accountants as Catalysts for Growth & SME IPOs"** at **Vigyan Bhawan, New Delhi.** Shared the stage with visionary leaders and emphasized how CAs can transform SME growth through financial leadership and IPO strategy.

National Workshop on Export Promotion – MSME Ministry, Govt. of India

Spoke on **funding strategies beyond traditional finance** at this government-organized seminar hosted by **MSME-DFO, Okhla, New Delhi.** Engaged with industry leaders and policymakers to explore export-driven growth and SME IPO readiness.

Utkarsh – National Conference

Delivering a keynote session on SME IPO strategy and funding opportunities at Utkarsh, a premier national conference for financial professionals.

Podcast with Mr. Jagmohan Singh

Explored the science behind SME IPOs and financial transformation on the Cash Flow Expert Podcast

NIRC of ICAI – Investor Awareness Seminar

As Guest Speaker, spoke on IPO readiness and investor attraction strategies at the Northern India Regional Council seminar.

SME IPO Kalpvriksh Online Session

Hosted a virtual session on IPO success formulas for SMEs, reaching hundreds of participants across India.

Kolkata Session – SME IPO and Growth

Engaged with business owners and professionals in Kolkata, sharing actionable strategies for business expansion via IPOs.

North EX CA Study Circle

Led a workshop on market trends and post-IPO financial structuring for SME clients.

Central Delhi Study Circle

Guided professionals on SME IPO compliance and valuation practices during a focused seminar in Central Delhi.

Karol Bagh Westens CPE Study Circle

Interactive session with fellow Chartered Accountants discussing compliance frameworks for SME listings.

PART 1:
WHY YOUR BUSINESS ISN'T GROWING (AND HOW TO FIX IT)

Stop Making Excuses. It's Time to Face the Truth.

If you've made it this far, congratulations—you've done something most business owners never do. You've admitted that **playing small isn't an option anymore.**

The last few pages probably **felt like a wake-up call**. Good. You needed that. You needed to see that the biggest thing keeping your business from scaling isn't a lack of money, connections, or market demand—it's **YOU.**

× Not the economy.

× Not your industry.

× Not the competition.

√ **YOU.**

You've been operating under the illusion that growth has to be **slow, safe, and small.** That if you just "grind hard enough" and "take things step by step," one day, you'll **magically** arrive at the top.

Spoiler alert: That's not how it works.

Your Dad's Business Model Won't Work in Today's Market.

You're stuck thinking like **your dad's generation.** And listen—that's not entirely a bad thing.

There's value in **old-school business wisdom**.

√ Being grounded.

√ Knowing your numbers.

√ Running lean.

That's what kept businesses alive for **decades.**

But here's the problem—**"Jitni chadar hai utne per failaiye"** (stretch your legs only as far as your blanket allows) may have been solid advice in their time, but if it were an absolute truth, companies like **Facebook, Zomato, Google, and Amazon** would have never become billion-dollar giants.

They didn't just stretch within their limits—they **expanded their chadar** by taking **calculated risks, leveraging external funding, and thinking exponentially, not just incrementally.**

The world has changed. Playing small won't get you big results anymore. **It's time to think beyond survival and start thinking about scale.**

Look... here's what you need to understand...

When your dad built his business, the world was **different.**

× No internet.

× No instant access to global markets.

× No AI rewriting industries overnight.

Back then, businesses had **time to grow.**

√ **Competition was local.**

√ **Scaling took decades.**

√ **You could afford to move slow.**

But today?

√ **Speed wins.**

√ **Attention wins.**

√ **Capital wins.**

And with AI revolutionizing everything from **logistics to customer service**, that speed is **only going to skyrocket.**

The businesses that **adapt fast and scale faster** will dominate. The ones that move slow? **They'll die.**

The Comfort Zone is a Death Trap

Most Indian businesses don't **fail** because they aren't capable. They **fail** because they stay **comfortable.**

Even **Prime Minister Modi has said this**: "If you stay in your comfort zone, you will never grow."

Think about it—what's your **comfort zone?**

→ A small business owner feels safe with **word-of-mouth sales.**

→ A **rickshaw driver** feels safe driving his usual route every day.

→ A **corporate employee** feels safe getting a **monthly salary.**

And then suddenly, something **disrupts** that comfort zone.

Think about **kirana stores**. They felt **safe** for decades.

Then BlinkIt, Swiggy Instamart, and Zepto showed up.

Suddenly, customers **stopped walking to the shop** because they could get groceries **delivered in 15 minutes.**

The stores that **adapted** and started online deliveries **survived.**

The ones that **stayed comfortable**? They **disappeared.**

This is why **staying small is a bigger risk than scaling.**

The same is true for YOUR business. If you're not moving forward, you're falling behind.

Real Business Growth Isn't a Slow Crawl. It's a Bold Leap.

Do you think Tata, Infosys, Reliance, or Zomato got where they are today by **"waiting for the right time"**?

No.

They became **giants** because they **made bold moves when others hesitated.**

And **right now**, you're at the same crossroads.

This section is where we **rip off the bandaid** and force you to face some **hard truths**:

You're thinking too small.

Your fear of losing control is suffocating your growth.

Relying on bank loans and private investors is keeping you poor.

But here's the **good news—awareness is the first step.**

Once you see the problem for what it is, you can **finally break free from it.**

The 4 Biggest Reasons Businesses Never Scale

1. **They rely on personal savings instead of smart capital. Personal savings limit growth.** If you're funding expansion from your own pocket, your business will only grow as much as your bank balance allows.

2. **They're obsessed with "owning 100%" instead of building something bigger. Ownership means nothing if the company isn't growing.**

3. **They treat debt like a lifeline instead of a trap. Debt alone will not accelerate your growth.**

Borrowing is fine in the short term, but there's always a ceiling—a limit to how much you can borrow before it starts suffocating your profits. Debt can keep your business afloat, but it won't take it to the next level.

4. **They refuse to admit they need a new strategy. Markets change. Technology evolves.** Businesses that fail to adapt get left behind. You can't scale if you're stuck using old-school funding methods while your competitors raise crores through IPOs.

Inside these next few chapters, I'm going to **shatter every excuse** you've ever made for **not scaling.**

The Harsh Truth: What Happens If Your Competitor Scales Before You?

Imagine this:

Your **direct competitor**—same industry, same market, same customers—**goes public before you.**

Here's what happens next:

√ They raise **₹50 crores in IPO funding.**

√ They **expand aggressively** into new cities.

√ They **offer better salaries** and steal your top employees.

√ They **launch aggressive marketing** and dominate your space.

You might think, **"This won't affect me. I'll just keep running my business as usual."** But **aankh band kar lene se andhera nahi hota**—closing your eyes to reality doesn't change what's happening around you.

Your competitor is **growing at lightning speed** while you're stuck playing defense. The market is moving forward, with or without you.

So the real question is: **Will you adapt and claim your share, or will you wait until there's nothing left to claim?**

This Section is Your Business Intervention.

The part where we **break through the myths and mental blocks** keeping you from **explosive growth.**

By the end of these next few chapters, you won't just **understand** why staying private is the **riskiest move of all—**you'll **feel it in your gut.**

You'll **never look at your business the same way again.**

Now let's do this.

CHAPTER - 1

THE BUSINESS KILLER – THINKING SMALL

Fear is Expensive - Why Avoiding an IPO Could Be the Costliest Mistake You Ever Make

What if I told you that the biggest threat to your business isn't the competition, market conditions, or lack of funding—but the way you think?

You see, small business owners don't fail because they lack potential.

They fail because they lack vision.

Most SMEs don't collapse overnight. They slowly wither away because their founders refuse to think beyond their comfort zones. They tell themselves, *"We're doing fine.*

We don't need to scale."

And then, one day, they wake up and realize:

√   Their competitors have outgrown them.

√   The market has changed.

√   Customers are moving on.

And Just Like That, Their *"Stable"* Business Becomes Obsolete.

This isn't just theory. It's happening right now.

The Silent Killer of Small Businesses: Playing It Safe

Let me tell you a story.

For decades, local kirana stores (small neighborhood grocery shops) were the backbone of Indian retail. They operated with a simple mindset—buy stock, sell at a small margin, and survive on repeat customers. It worked. Until it didn't.

Enter **Zepto**, the 10-minute grocery delivery startup. While kirana stores relied on the same old methods, Zepto did something different—they **scaled fast** with investor funding.

√   They raised $1.95B (₹16,185 crores) in funding.

√   They built a hyper-efficient supply chain.

√   They acquired customers through aggressive marketing.

√   They used tech to make grocery delivery faster than ever before.

Result? Kirana stores, which were once untouchable, suddenly found themselves **losing customers**. While they stuck to their comfort zones, Zepto **expanded aggressively**—launching in multiple cities and raising even more capital.

And here's the kicker—Zepto isn't **profitable** yet. But investors are backing it because of its **growth potential**. Meanwhile, kirana stores that refused to modernize are shutting down.

The lesson? **Thinking small is riskier than thinking big.**

This isn't just happening in retail. The same pattern plays out in **every** industry. Those who hesitate to scale get left behind. Those who take bold steps and secure funding **dominate the market**.

But let's look at the other side of the story—what happens when a business **relies too much on debt** and collapses under its weight?

The Debt Trap That Took Down Reliance Communications

Debt can be a powerful tool for business growth—but if mismanaged, it can destroy even the biggest companies.

In the early 2000s, **Anil Ambani's Reliance Communications (RCom)** was a telecom giant. It had a massive market share, strong customer base, and everything going for it.

But there was a problem—**the company was drowning in debt**.

√ In 2010, RCom had ₹28,000 crore in debt.

√ By 2019, this ballooned to ₹48,500 crore.

√ The company **couldn't keep up with interest payments**.

Meanwhile, Mukesh Ambani's **Reliance Jio** played a different game. Instead of **relying on debt**, they **secured massive investor funding** and built the infrastructure for India's telecom revolution.

√ Jio invested ₹150,000 crore into its network.

√ It offered free voice calls and dirt-cheap data.

√ It secured investments from global giants like **Google and Facebook**.

The result? **Jio crushed the competition.**

RCom, drowning in debt, had no money left to compete. It **shut down its wireless operations in 2017** and filed for **bankruptcy in 2019**.

Meanwhile, **Reliance Jio is now a ₹9 lakh crore company**.

The Lesson?

If you want to scale, **you can't rely only on debt**. The businesses that win **use public funding (IPOs), private investors, and strategic expansion**—not just bank loans that eat away profits.

And that's exactly why smart entrepreneurs go public.

The Most Expensive Decision You'll Ever Make? Not Going Public.

You think an IPO is too complicated?

You think your business is too small?

You think you're not ready?

Let's destroy those myths right now.

Because here's the truth: **staying small is costing you more than you realize.**

The Real Cost of Thinking Small

1. **Lost Market Share: Ola's Delayed IPO & Uber's Domination**

    Ola was once **India's #1 ride-hailing platform**, even outpacing Uber in market penetration. But they made one critical mistake: **they delayed their IPO**—multiple times.

    While Ola struggled with regulatory challenges and capital constraints, Uber **expanded aggressively in India**, leveraging its global financial strength.

The result?

√   **Uber took market share, dominating metro cities.**

√   **Ola had to raise expensive private funding instead of public capital.**

√   **Its valuation fluctuated, and investor confidence weakened.**

    Ola's delay meant it lost **first-mover advantage in IPO-driven expansion**, giving Uber the edge.

2. **Missed Funding Opportunities: A Delayed IPO = Slower Growth**

    While you struggle with cash flow, IPO-backed competitors are expanding, hiring, and innovating.

Look at **DroneAcharya Aerial Innovations**—a Pune-based drone-tech company.

Before their IPO? A **small operation**. After raising ₹34 crore through an SME IPO in 2022?

√ **Expanded their training and R&D operations.**

√ **Stock jumped 94% post-listing.**

√ **They're now a leader in India's drone tech revolution.**

Meanwhile, competitors that relied on slow capital-raising methods **are still waiting for approvals and lagging behind**.

3. **No Exit Strategy: What's Your Plan?**

   What's your long-term plan? Are you just going to keep grinding for decades and hope for the best?

   An IPO gives you **liquidity**—a way to **cash out while growing**.

   Example?

√ **Likhitha Infrastructure Ltd** (Oil & Gas Pipelines) – Raised ₹61 crore in 2020, expanded, and gave early investors an **exit at a 300% return** within a year.

√ **Senco Gold & Diamonds** – Family-run for 80 years, but its **₹405 crore IPO in 2023** positioned it as a **national luxury brand** instead of a regional jeweler.

These businesses didn't wait until they were "big enough." They became big **because they took the bold step first**.

Here's the thing… IPO-Backed Companies Win.

Every industry has two kinds of businesses:

√ **Those who take funding seriously and scale.**

√ **Those who hesitate and get left behind.**

The choice is yours.

The Common Myths That Keep Indian Entrepreneurs From Going Public (And Why They're Wrong)

Myth - "An IPO is only for billion-dollar companies."

→ Wrong. SME IPOs exist specifically for businesses like yours—₹3 Cr to ₹25 Cr PAT in size.

Myth - "I'll lose control of my company."

→ No, you won't. You'll raise funds without selling your soul to VCs who demand a say in your business.

Myth - "It's too complicated."

→ That's what experts like me are for. The process is structured, and thousands of SMEs have done it successfully.

Myth - "What if it doesn't work?"

→ What if it does? What if you raise enough to 10X your business while your competitors are still taking bank loans?

The Harsh Truth: If You're Not Growing, You're Dying

Here's something you need to understand:

An IPO isn't just about money. It's about **momentum.**

√ It gets you **capital**.

√ It builds your **brand**.

√ It opens doors to **new customers, bigger deals, and better employees.**

But let's address something that no one talks about—the hidden resistance that could be holding you back. And it's not coming from competitors, banks, or investors. It's coming from home.

Breaking the Fear: Aligning Your Family with Your Growth

If you're a business owner, you already know this—your family sees everything.

They see the long nights, the stressful days, the endless problem-solving. They see you sacrificing comfort, stability, and peace of mind just to keep things running.

So when you tell them, "I'm thinking of expanding the business and taking it public," their first thought isn't excitement.

It's fear.

They think, "If he's already under so much stress, won't a bigger business just make it worse?"

They're not wrong to worry. But they're looking at it the wrong way.

The truth is, scaling the right way **reduces** stress—it doesn't increase it. A business that remains small and underfunded forces the owner to **handle everything alone**—cash flow, growth, hiring, expansion, and day-to-day operations. But when you raise capital through an IPO, you **free yourself** from that financial strain. You can **hire a stronger team, automate processes, and delegate** instead of burning yourself out.

But here's the challenge—you can't expect your family to understand this on their own. They need guidance. And this is where having an **IPO expert** by your side makes all the difference.

An IPO expert doesn't just help you go public; they **help align your family with your vision**. They explain:

√   Why an IPO makes business **easier**, not harder.

√   How public funding helps you **reduce** financial stress.

√ How a well-planned IPO allows you to **spend more time with family**, not less.

Most importantly, they reassure your loved ones that **you're not risking everything**—you're taking a strategic step toward stability and freedom.

So if your family is hesitant, bring them into the conversation early. Let them understand the long-term benefits, not just the short-term concerns. **Because real business success isn't just about numbers—it's about securing a better future for yourself and the people who matter most.**

And while you're still debating whether to scale or not, something else is happening in the background.

Your competitors? They aren't waiting.

√ They're hiring the best talent **(before you can afford them).**

Why? Because listed companies have a massive advantage—you don't just offer salaries, you offer ESOPs (Employee Stock Option Plans). The best employees don't just want a paycheck; they want ownership, long-term wealth, and job security. A listed company can attract high-caliber talent by offering stock options, something a private business cannot compete with.

√ They're scaling their operations **(while you're still bootstrapping).**

How? IPO-backed businesses have instant access to capital for expansion—they don't have to wait years to reinvest profits or take on risky loans. This means they can **open new branches, increase production, invest in technology, or enter new markets** while you're still stuck negotiating with banks or trying to self-fund your next move.

√ They're buying out smaller competitors **(like you).**

What happens when your competitor has more cash? They acquire companies, eliminate competition, and dominate market share. If your industry is fragmented, they will buy businesses like yours, consolidate the market, and take control. A public company has the financial muscle to acquire smaller private firms that are struggling to scale— meaning if you're not growing fast enough, you might become their next acquisition target.

Want to keep running a comfortable, small business? That's fine.

But don't complain when someone with **half your experience, half your skills, and half your potential surpasses you**—not because they're smarter, but because they had the guts to scale.

Because **growth isn't supposed to be easy**.

Instagram reels? Saral (easy).

Reading a book? Sahi (right).

Saral and Sahi are never the same thing. The right path is rarely the easy one.

And in business, the **right move is to scale—even if it's uncomfortable**.

The Shift You Need to Make—Today

So, what's the mindset shift every Indian business owner needs?

Stop thinking of your business as a small, personal venture. Start thinking of it as a scalable empire.

Stop fearing the IPO process. Start embracing it as your fastest path to explosive growth.

Stop waiting for the "right time." The right time was yesterday. The next best time is NOW.

Because here's the ugly truth:

The world is changing fast. AI is disrupting industries. Competition is fiercer than ever.

The old, slow way of growing a business **won't work anymore.**

The only businesses that will survive and thrive are the ones that **move quickly, raise capital smartly, and leverage public funding to dominate their industries.**

And that?

That starts **with you.**

Checklist: The Mindset Shift Every Indian Business Owner Needs

√ Growth isn't optional—it's survival.

√ If you're not scaling, your competitors are.

√ Thinking small is the #1 reason businesses fail.

√ An IPO isn't about losing control—it's about gaining power.

√ Your business doesn't have to be huge to go public. It has to be ready.

√ The best time to start preparing for an IPO was yesterday. The next best time is today.

Final Words Before You Turn the Page

Look, I don't care if you're skeptical.

I don't care if you think an IPO isn't for you.

What I care about is whether you're **willing to stay small forever.**

Because that's what's at stake here.

If you keep waiting, hesitating, and doubting—you'll watch your industry move forward while you stay stuck.

But if you **make the mindset shift**—if you start thinking like a business that **deserves** to scale—then the possibilities are endless.

So, what's it going to be?

Stay small—or **build an empire?**

The choice is yours.

Get 1-on-1 IPO strategy advice on WhatsApp.

CHAPTER - 2

THE #1 EXCUSE – "BUT I'LL LOSE CONTROL!"

Let's Debunk This Lie Right Now

Every business owner wants to stay in control. It's natural. You built this company from the ground up. You've sacrificed sleep, comfort, and maybe even your sanity to get it where it is today.

So when someone tells you to take your company public, your first thought is:

"What if I lose control?"

"What if investors start dictating how I run my business?"

"What if I end up just being a figurehead in my own company?"

These are valid fears. But here's the truth that no one is telling you:

The businesses that stay private in fear of losing control... actually lose control faster.

Why?

Because they run out of money. Because they're stuck in slow growth. Because their competitors—who had the guts to raise public capital—**crush them.**

If you're making decisions out of fear instead of strategy, **you've already lost control.**

Let's fix that.

The Ego Trap—How Staying Private Is Actually Costing You Money

You think holding 100% of your company is the smartest move? Think again.

You know who holds 100% of their company?

Small business owners who never scale.

You know who holds 40%, 30%, or even just 20% of their company? Business owners who have built giants.

Take a second and do the math.

Would you rather own **100% of a ₹10 crore company?**

Or would you rather own **70% of a ₹500 crore company?**

The answer is obvious.

Wealth isn't about ownership. It's about growth.

Here's how the most successful businesses in India actually operate:

√ **They use investor money to scale** instead of draining their personal funds.

√ **They attract top talent** by offering stock incentives.

√ **They expand aggressively** while others "wait for the right time."

√ **They understand that ownership percentage means nothing** if the business isn't growing.

Meanwhile, private companies stay stuck:

× Struggling with high-interest loans.

× Struggling with limited expansion.

× Struggling to convince top talent to join them.

See the problem?

Real Story: The Control Myth That Almost Killed Infosys

Let me take you back to the early days of Infosys.

In 1981, **Narayan Murthy and six other co-founders** started Infosys with just ₹10,000, borrowed from Murthy's wife. They had big ambitions but limited resources. For years, they grew slowly, relying on private funding, client contracts, and personal savings.

By the early 1990s, Infosys had an opportunity to **scale massively**. But they needed capital—**real capital**.

At that time, many Indian businesses avoided IPOs. The fear was the same: **"We'll lose control."**

One of Infosys's early co-founders was hesitant. He wanted the company to stay private, fearing that external investors would interfere with their decision-making. He argued that keeping control meant staying safe.

Murthy saw things differently.

He knew that without **fresh capital**, Infosys would remain a mid-sized software company—just another IT service provider in a sea of competitors. So he made the bold move.

In 1993, Infosys went public. They raised ₹16.58 crore—**peanuts by today's standards, but life-changing for them.**

That IPO changed everything.

√   They gained credibility.

√   They expanded internationally.

√   They attracted **top-tier talent**.

√   They became the **face of India's IT revolution**.

And what happened to the co-founder who feared losing control?

He sold his shares and **left the company in 1994.**

By 1999, **Infosys became the first Indian company to be listed on the NASDAQ**. By 2024, its valuation had **crossed ₹6.5 lakh crore.**

Meanwhile, the co-founder who exited too early **missed out on what could have been a fortune beyond imagination.**

That's what happens when **you choose control over growth**.

Why Giving Up a Piece of the Pie Actually Makes You Richer

If your company is worth **₹10 crore today**, and you go public, raise **₹100 crore**, and scale it into a **₹500 crore empire**—do you really think you've "lost" anything?

Let me give you a **simple analogy**.

Imagine you have **10 chapatis on your plate**.

But to satisfy your hunger, **you only need two**.

What do you do with the remaining **eight**?

- **Option 1:** Hoard them, even if you don't need them, while they go stale.
- **Option 2:** Share them wisely—feed others, build relationships, and gain influence.

Your company's ownership works the same way.

To stay in control, **you don't need 100%—you only need 51%**. That's the number that keeps you in charge.

So, **why not give up 49% at the right time, to the right people, for the right valuation?**

By raising public capital, you're not "losing" anything—you're gaining:

√   **More money to scale.**

√   **Higher valuation.**

√   **A stronger, more dominant business.**

Holding onto 100% of a ₹10 crore company isn't wealth. Holding 51% of a ₹500 crore company is.

The Reliance IPO: A Masterclass in Raising Smart Capital

Let's talk about one of the most iconic IPO success stories in India—**Reliance Industries**.

When Dhirubhai Ambani started Reliance, banks refused to give him loans. They didn't believe in his vision. They saw his company as just another textile business—not the future giant it was destined to be.

But Ambani didn't let traditional funding barriers stop him.

Instead of **begging banks for money**, he turned to **the Indian public**.

In 1977, Reliance went public.

Thousands of middle-class Indians—who had never invested in stocks before—put their trust (and money) into the company.

And what happened next?

√   Reliance scaled rapidly, entering new industries.

√   It gained credibility, making future capital raises easier.

√   It went from being a small business to an empire.

Today, **Reliance is worth over ₹18 lakh crore**, dominating industries from telecom to energy.

And it all started because they **chose public funding over bank loans.**

But what if they hadn't?

What if they had waited? What if they had let fear stop them?

Imagine a world where Reliance **never went public**.

Where they stayed small, struggling to get loans, missing out on expansion opportunities.

That's the reality for thousands of businesses today. Not because they lack potential—**but because they hesitate.**

The Irony of Fear

You fear losing control... but **right now, you're the one limiting your company's potential.**

You're terrified of bringing in outside investors... but **your bank already controls how much capital you can access and at what cost.**

You think you can maintain control by staying private... but **staying private means staying small.**

It's not the IPO that steals control from you. It's inaction.

The "Private" vs. "Public" Business War

Here's a scenario you need to think about.

Imagine you're running **an auto parts manufacturing business**. You've got ₹3-4 crore of Profit-After-Tax (PAT). Business is okay, but you're stuck. You need more capital to scale, but bank loans come with crushing interest rates.

Meanwhile, your competitor—a similar-sized company—goes public.

√   They raise ₹15 crore from the public market.

√   They expand production.

√   They strike a deal with an international auto giant.

√   They hire top-tier talent that you couldn't afford.

√   Their valuation **skyrockets**.

What happens next?

Within 3 years, they dominate the industry, and your company is barely holding on.

That's the real risk.

Losing "control" by going public?

or Losing your **market position** because your competitor raised capital before you?

Think about it.

If you don't take this step now, your competitor will. And by the time you realize it, **it'll be too late.**

Public Companies = More Control, Not Less

This might sound contradictory, but let me explain:

Public companies actually have MORE control over their growth than private companies.

How?

Access to unlimited capital. Need funds to scale? You can raise it—without paying high-interest rates to a bank.

Stronger brand credibility. Investors and customers trust public companies more than private ones.

Better hiring power. The best talent wants to work for companies with stock options and long-term growth.

Freedom from banks and private lenders. No more begging for business loans.

Going public doesn't mean giving up power. It means gaining leverage.

How Much Longer Will You Let Fear Hold You Back?

If you take away just one thing from this chapter, let it be this:

√ **Going public doesn't make you lose control. It gives you MORE control over your future.**

√ **You don't need to own 100% of your business. You need to own a business that's actually growing.**

√ **The longer you wait, the more ground you lose.**

The biggest mistake you can make is waiting until it's too late.

Checklist: 3 Things to Do TODAY to Shift Your Thinking

√ **Stop fearing investor involvement.** You still call the shots—the only difference is, you now have the capital to execute bigger moves.

√ **Calculate what your company could be worth if it had IPO-level funding.** If you don't know the number, find out.

√ **Ask yourself:** Would I rather own **100% of a ₹10 Cr company, or 70% of a ₹100 Cr company?** If your answer is still the first one, **you're thinking too small.**

Get 1-on-1 IPO strategy advice on WhatsApp.

CHAPTER - 3

WHY RELYING ON LOANS IS KEEPING YOU POOR

The Hard Truth About Business Funding

You've got big plans for your business. Scaling. Expansion. Dominating your market. But when it comes to **funding that growth**, most small business owners turn to the same **three losing strategies**:

√ Taking **bank loans** and drowning in interest payments.

√ Giving up equity to **VCs** and losing control over decision-making.

√ Burning through **personal savings** and limiting growth potential.

If you're doing **any** of these, you're keeping yourself **poor**.

I get it. **Funding is a nightmare for Indian SMEs.** Banks make you beg for capital, investors want massive control, and personal savings can only take you so far.

But here's what most business owners **don't realize**:

There's a **better way.** A way to **raise capital without losing control**, a way to **expand without debt eating your margins**, a way to **grow without relying on the whims of VCs.**

That way? **An IPO.**

Let's break it down.

Why Bank Loans Are Killing Your Profits

For decades, **bank loans have been the go-to option** for Indian businesses. Need money? **Go to the bank.**

Simple, right?

Wrong.

Because every rupee you **borrow** from a bank comes with one thing attached—**interest**. And that interest? **It's eating away at your profits every single day.**

Let's put this into perspective:

A ₹**10 crore loan** with a **12% interest rate** means you're paying ₹**1.2 crore per year**—just in interest. That's ₹**1.2 crore** that could've gone into **scaling your business, hiring better talent, or expanding operations**.

Instead? **You're just working to pay off the bank.**

And the worst part? **The bank owns you.**

The Dark Side of Borrowing: The Café Coffee Day Story

Now, let's flip the script.

Not all businesses that take bank loans survive. Some drown in debt.

Take **Café Coffee Day (CCD).**

V.G. Siddhartha, the founder of CCD, had a wildly successful coffee chain. It was growing. Expanding. But behind the scenes, there was a **debt spiral that was slowly killing the business.**

Heavy borrowing.

Crippling interest payments.

Constant pressure from lenders.

When COVID hit and revenues dropped, the debt didn't stop. CCD kept bleeding cash.

The financial stress became **too much**. Tragically, Siddhartha took his own life in 2019, leaving behind a company on the brink of collapse.

Siddhartha's story is a brutal reminder:

Bank loans don't care about market conditions. When a crisis hits, your EMI doesn't stop.

Debt can become a death sentence for businesses.

But if not bank loans, then what?

Many business owners believe the only other option is venture capital funding.

But here's the hidden truth—**VCs can be just as dangerous as bank loans.**

Before we talk about the IPO alternative, let's take a hard look at how VC funding actually works.

Venture Capitalists: The "Investors" Who Steal Your Company

VC funding sounds **great on paper**. Get investors, raise capital, scale fast.

But here's what **they won't tell you** until it's **too late**:

√ **VCs don't invest to grow your business.** They invest to **take control**.

√ **They pressure you for aggressive growth,** even if it's **bad for your business.**

√ **They want an exit strategy,** not **long-term success.**

Here's how it usually plays out:

1. They invest in your company, take a **huge chunk of equity**.

2. They **push for crazy fast expansion**, whether your business is ready or not.

3. They **pressure you to sell or go public—but on their terms, not yours**.

4. By the time you **realize it**, you're **no longer the owner of your own business**.

Sound extreme? It's not.

Ask **any founder** who's taken VC money, and they'll tell you—**once you let investors in, you're no longer the boss.**

You **started your company** to **build a legacy**, not to **build wealth for some investor sitting in Mumbai, Delhi, or Silicon Valley**.

VCs **don't care** about your business. They **care about their return**.

So if you think **bank loans** are bad, **VC funding is worse**.

And here's the irony—**VCs don't invest because they believe in long-term business ownership. Most venture capitalists fund startups that aren't IPO-ready**, helping them survive only until they can scale enough to be acquired or go public.

For VCs, an IPO isn't a growth plan—it's an exit plan.

The IPO Solution: Raising Capital WITHOUT Losing Control

So, if **bank loans are a trap** and **VC funding is a ticking time bomb**, what's the alternative?

An IPO.

√ You raise capital from the public, NOT from banks or VCs.

√   You don't pay interest, so your profits stay yours.

√   You still call the shots—investors don't run your business.

√   Your business gets instant credibility and a higher valuation.

While most businesses struggle between loans and VC funding, some take the smarter route—an IPO.

Mankind Pharma is a perfect example. Instead of giving up control to private investors, they built a billion-dollar empire by leveraging public markets.

How Mankind Pharma Became a Billion-Dollar Giant Without VCs

Mankind Pharma—one of India's largest pharmaceutical companies—**could have taken the easy way out.**

In the 2000s, they had multiple offers from **venture capital firms** willing to invest millions. **But they said NO.**

Why?

Because they didn't want to **lose control** of their business.

Instead of selling out to VCs, they **focused on organic growth** and **raising funds through smarter financial strategies**.

And in **2023**, they finally **went public**, raising ₹4,326 crore in one of the biggest IPOs of the year.

Today, Mankind Pharma is worth over ₹96,000 crore, still controlled by its founders—**without ever giving in to VC pressure**.

Lesson: If a company can scale into a **multi-billion-dollar empire** without selling its soul to VCs, **so can you.**

That's a billion-dollar success story, but what about smaller businesses?

You might be thinking—"I don't run a massive pharmaceutical empire." Fair. But IPOs aren't just for big corporations. Even small and medium-sized enterprises (SMEs) have used IPOs to break free from financial struggles.

Meet Hamps Bio Limited.

Case Study: How an Indian SME Broke Free from Debt with an IPO

A small Indian company with a **turnover of just ₹6.5 crore and a profit of ₹50 lakh**.

A few years ago, they were **stuck in the same cycle** as most SMEs:

→ **Limited growth.**

→ **Struggling with cash flow.**

→ **Unable to expand because banks wouldn't loan more.**

They had two choices:

1. Take a **bank loan** and pay **high-interest rates.**

2. Sell equity to **private investors** and **lose control.**

Instead, they made a **bold move—they went public.**

They raised ₹6 crore from investors.

They expanded operations, doubled production.

Their market valuation skyrocketed.

Today, they're **worth far more** than they ever imagined—**all without being shackled to a bank or controlled by private investors.**

This isn't just one success story.

√ **Avax Apparels & Ornaments Limited** raised **₹1.92 crore** through an SME IPO.

√ **Over 100+ SME IPOs** have listed in India, raising **crores for expansion.**

√ **As of Dec 2024, hundreds of SMEs** have gone public, **gaining financial freedom.**

These companies are **NOT tech giants**. They are **NOT billion-dollar corporations.**

They're **just like you.**

The only difference?

They bet on themselves.

The Choice Is Simple: Keep Struggling or Go Big

At this point, **you have two choices.**

Keep relying on bank loans and watch **interest drain your profits.**

Keep chasing VC funding and **give up control of your business.**

Or go public, raise smart capital, and build a business that dominates.

Going public isn't just about money. It's about freedom.

Freedom from banks... Freedom from investor pressure... Freedom to scale YOUR way.

The biggest mistake you can make is waiting too long.

By the time you finally decide, **your competitors might have already taken the leap**—and they'll be **five steps ahead of you.**

Checklist: Which Funding Method Is Actually Right for You?

√ **Do you want full control over how your business scales?**
  → An IPO is your best option.

√ **Do you want to avoid long-term interest payments eating into profits?** → Avoid bank loans.

√ **Do you want to raise capital without investors dictating every move?** → VCs are NOT for you.

An IPO isn't the finish line—it's the starting line to building your empire.

Scan the QR Code → Answer a Few Simple Questions →

Get a Custom Eligibility Check Report from Our Expert Team.

PART 2:
WHY IPOS ARE A CHEAT CODE FOR BUILDING EMPIRES

The Fast Track to Market Domination Starts Here

By now, you've seen what's holding most businesses back.

You've uncovered the silent killers—**small thinking, fear of losing control, and outdated funding strategies that keep businesses stuck.** You've seen how most SMEs remain trapped in survival mode, constantly battling cash flow problems, relying on loans that drain profits, and fearing that going public will mean losing control.

Now, it's time to shift focus.

This section is where we **stop talking about roadblocks and start talking about acceleration.** Because the truth is, businesses that hesitate, waiting for the "perfect moment" to scale, are already being left behind by those who are bold enough to leverage the power of public funding.

Let's be clear: **An IPO isn't just about raising money.**

It's about **transformation.**

It's about **positioning yourself as an industry leader.**

It's about **creating a ripple effect that sets your business on a path to unstoppable growth.**

Here's what's coming next:

- **You'll discover the untold truths about IPOs**—why companies that list **instantly gain credibility, attract bigger opportunities, and command industry-wide respect.** You'll see why businesses that stay private are stuck in slow motion while publicly listed companies **unlock doors that most entrepreneurs don't even know exist.**

- **We'll break down how an IPO sets off a chain reaction**—how one bold move **fuels faster scaling, attracts elite talent, and gives you access to resources that private businesses simply can't match.** The moment a company goes public, its valuation shifts, its market perception changes, and it becomes an entirely different force in the industry. You'll learn why a listed company is taken more seriously by customers, vendors, and investors alike.

- **Finally, we dive into market domination**—how small companies have leveraged IPOs to **skyrocket their valuations, expand aggressively, and outpace competitors who once seemed untouchable.** We'll analyze how businesses that were once seen as minor players turned themselves into industry giants, simply because they understood how to leverage public funding at the right time.

Think about the businesses you admire. The ones that lead their industries. The ones that have national—and even global—presence. They didn't get there by waiting. They didn't sit around trying to grow incrementally with limited capital and old-school methods. They took the leap. They used public funding as a launchpad to go from "small player" to market leader.

This is the turning point.

But here's the thing—an IPO isn't just about external perception.

It changes the way you operate internally. With funding, you can hire the best talent in the market, professionals who don't just work for a paycheck but build legacies. You can expand faster, reach customers you never had access to, and make strategic acquisitions that strengthen your market position.

While others are stuck trying to save costs and survive, listed companies have the **power to invest in growth.**

You've already seen what happens when businesses hesitate.

Now, it's time to see what happens when **businesses go all in and change the game.**

Because the companies that scale fast will own the future.

The only question is—will yours be one of them?

Turn the page—your empire is waiting.

CHAPTER - 4

SEVEN BRUTAL TRUTHS ABOUT IPOs EVERY BUSINESS OWNER NEEDS TO KNOW

The Harsh Reality: What No One Tells You About IPOs

If you're reading this, you're already ahead of 99% of business owners. You're not just thinking about growth—you're thinking about **real scale.** And if you're serious about taking your business to the next level, there's one thing you need to do first:

Forget everything you think you know about IPOs.

Most business owners dismiss the idea of going public because of myths, fears, or misinformation. They assume IPOs are only for billion-dollar corporations. They think it's too complicated, too risky, or just **not for them.**

The truth? IPOs aren't just for the Tatas and Reliances of the world. They're for **any business owner who's serious about growth.**

And in this chapter, we're going to break down the **seven brutal truths** about IPOs—truths that could completely change how you see your business.

Brutal Truth #1: Your Business Will NEVER Grow Beyond a Certain Point Without Public Funding

Here's a fact most business owners don't want to hear: **If you don't raise capital, your business will hit a ceiling.**

It doesn't matter how great your product is. It doesn't matter how hard you work. If you don't have the funds to scale, you're stuck.

Think about it:

- How do you expand into new markets? **Money.**
- How do you hire top talent? **Money.**
- How do you invest in better technology, marketing, and infrastructure? **Money.**

And here's the problem—**your business profits alone are not enough to fund massive expansion.**

Sure, you might grow slowly over 10, 15, or 20 years. But by then, your competitors—who **raised funds the smart way**—will already be dominating the market.

Brutal Truth #2: If You Don't Go Public, Your Competitor Will

The market doesn't wait for you. If you hesitate, someone else will take the leap before you.

Let's talk about **Zomato vs. Swiggy**—a classic example of how **going public at the right time can change the game.**

Zomato went public in **2021**, raising ₹9,375 crore. With fresh capital, they went on an **aggressive expansion spree**, acquiring competitors and strengthening their market position. They didn't just raise money; they gained credibility, investor confidence, and a massive war chest to outspend competitors.

Meanwhile, **Swiggy stayed private for years**, relying on venture capital to fund its growth. This meant **constant pressure from investors, limited resources, and slower expansion** compared to Zomato's post-IPO scaling.

However, in **2024, Swiggy finally decided to go public**, filing for a **₹10,400 crore IPO** to compete on equal footing. But here's the key takeaway—**by the time they listed, Zomato had already solidified its lead**.

The Lesson?

Had Swiggy gone public earlier, they **could have accelerated their growth sooner**. Delaying the decision meant **playing catch-up while their biggest rival raced ahead**.

If you don't raise public funds, **your competitor will**—and when they do, they'll **outspend, out-hire, and outgrow you**.

Brutal Truth #3: Hiring Top Talent is 10X Easier for Public Companies

Want to attract the best minds in your industry? Going public is your golden ticket.

When you're a private company, your hiring pitch sounds like this:

"Join our company, and we'll pay you a salary."

But when you're a **public** company, your pitch sounds like this:

"Join us, and we'll not only pay you a salary, but you'll also get stock options that could make you rich."

ESOPs (Employee Stock Ownership Plans) are one of the biggest hiring advantages of public companies.

Look at what **Infosys did in the early 2000s**:

They started offering ESOPs to employees.

Suddenly, **top-tier talent from IITs and IIMs started joining them.**

Those stock options **turned early employees into millionaires.**

Infosys **grew faster** than competitors who couldn't offer equity-based incentives.

Today, **any company serious about hiring the best minds needs to offer stock options.** And to do that, **you need to be public.**

But ESOPs aren't the only reason why employees **prefer public companies over private ones. Listed companies provide job security, financial stability, and career growth opportunities** that private companies often can't match.

- **Transparency & Stability:** Public companies operate under strict financial regulations, ensuring employees aren't blindsided by sudden financial troubles or shutdowns.

- **Career Growth & Recognition:** Employees at listed companies benefit from higher visibility, industry recognition, and structured promotion paths.

- **Stock Liquidity & Wealth Creation:** Unlike private firms, **where stock options may have no real value until an acquisition**, listed companies provide employees with the chance to build wealth through stock appreciation and dividends.

In short, **talented professionals don't just chase high salaries—they chase long-term financial security.** And that's exactly why they prefer public companies over private ones.

Brutal Truth #4: An IPO Builds Instant Trust and Brand Power

Being a **listed** company automatically gives your brand credibility.

Imagine two companies competing for the same deal. One is private, and one is listed on the stock exchange. Who do you think **banks, investors, and big clients** trust more?

Being public tells the world:

√   You're **transparent** (your financials are audited and public).

√   You're **stable** (otherwise, the market wouldn't invest in you).

√   You're **scalable** (because only companies with real growth potential go public).

This is why even small businesses that go public **suddenly start attracting bigger clients** and bigger deals.

Brutal Truth #5: Relying on Private Investors Will Keep You Stuck

Think venture capital is a good alternative to an IPO? Think again.

VCs don't care about your long-term success. They care about their exit strategy.

The moment they invest in your company, they're already planning how to cash out. And that means:

- They'll **pressure you for short-term growth** even if it hurts your long-term vision.

- They'll **force decisions** that benefit them, not you.

- They'll **demand board seats** and take over decision-making.

An IPO, on the other hand, lets you raise funds without selling your soul.

Brutal Truth #6: The "Too Late" Trap – When Waiting Kills Businesses

One of the biggest mistakes entrepreneurs make? **Waiting too long to go public.**

They wait for **"better financials,"** for the **"perfect market conditions,"** or until their **"business is big enough."** And in that waiting, they lose **speed, market share, and investor confidence.**

Take **Ola** as an example.

It delayed its IPO multiple times, hoping to time the market perfectly. Meanwhile, Uber continued expanding aggressively, strengthening its dominance.

By the time Ola finally made its move, it had **lost significant market share** and faced increased competition.

Contrast this with **Zomato, Nykaa, and MapmyIndia**, who **acted fast**, listed at the right time, and unlocked **massive growth capital**—allowing them to outpace their competitors.

The truth?

The "perfect time" to go public doesn't exist.

The only bad IPO timing… is waiting too long.

Brutal Truth #7: Going Public is the Only Way to Play the Long Game

If you're serious about building a **legacy business**, an IPO isn't optional—it's necessary.

Reliance, Infosys, HDFC, Titan—every major Indian business that dominates today took the IPO route.

Why?

Because they understood that **public capital isn't just money—it's momentum.**

√   It fuels expansion.

√   It creates brand trust.

√   It lets businesses outgrow their competition.

And now, it's your turn.

Checklist: Why You Should Have Gone Public YESTERDAY

√   **Your business needs capital to grow, but you don't want to rely on banks or private investors.**

√   **You want to hire top-tier talent but can't compete with listed companies offering ESOPs.**

√   **You want instant credibility that attracts bigger deals, partners, and clients.**

√   **You're tired of slow growth and want to scale like the industry giants.**

Still hesitating?

Let me leave you with one last question:

If you don't go public, and your competitor does—where will your business be five years from now?

It's time to make a move.

Exclusive Workshop:

How IPOs Actually Work

CHAPTER - 5

THE IPO DOMINO EFFECT – HOW GOING PUBLIC TRANSFORMS YOUR ENTIRE BUSINESS

The Hidden Benefit of an IPO That No One Talks About

Most business owners think of an IPO as just **a way to raise money.** They assume it's about collecting funds and using them to grow. But here's what most people don't realize:

An IPO doesn't just inject money into your business—it transforms your entire company.

Once you go public, **everything** changes. Your brand, your hiring power, your access to capital, your ability to scale—it all goes into overdrive.

This is called **the IPO Domino Effect.**

You take one step—going public—and suddenly, a chain reaction of opportunities unfolds that weren't available before.

√   Your brand gets instant credibility.

√   You attract investors who want to fund your growth.

√   Top talent wants to work for you.

√   Banks offer you better loan terms (yes, banks start chasing YOU instead).

√   Your valuation skyrockets.

One move sets off a cascade of wins that change your business forever.

Before the IPO: A Constant Struggle for Capital

For most businesses, pre-IPO funding is a nightmare. They're forced to rely on personal savings, high-interest bank loans, or venture capital that comes with strings attached. Look at how most SMEs fund their growth before going public:

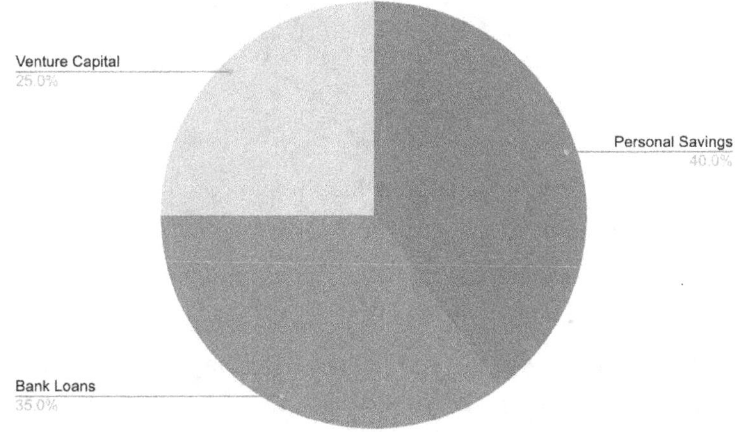

- 40% of funding comes from personal savings, meaning founders are taking on all the risk.

- 35% comes from bank loans, which drain cash flow through high-interest payments.

- 25% comes from venture capital, but it often leads to loss of control over business decisions.

- 0% from public markets—because they haven't tapped into IPO funding yet.

After the IPO: Financial Freedom and Smart Growth

Now, compare this to what happens after a company goes public:

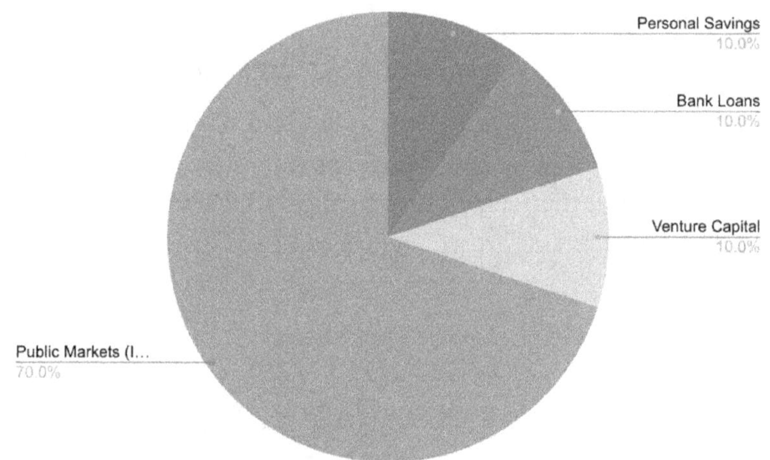

- Personal savings contribute just 10%—founders no longer need to risk their own capital.

- Bank loans are reduced to 10%—with public capital available, there's no need to rely on debt.

- VC funding drops to just 10%—because companies have raised money from the public instead.

- IPO funding now makes up 70%*—allowing for expansion, hiring, and long-term growth without financial stress.

*__Important Note:__ Raising 70% of funds through an IPO **does NOT mean giving up 70% ownership**. Most IPOs involve **only a fraction of equity dilution**, keeping majority control with the founders while unlocking massive capital for growth.

This shift is why IPOs **aren't just about raising money—they're about transforming how businesses operate.** The moment you go public, you gain access to long-term, low-risk funding.

How D-Mart's IPO Turned It Into a Retail Giant

In 2002, **Avenue Supermarts (D-Mart)** was just another retail chain in India. It had a solid business model—offering groceries and essentials at lower prices than competitors—but it wasn't a national brand yet.

For years, D-Mart relied on **internal funds** and slow expansion. But in 2017, it made a **game-changing decision**—it went public.

That IPO set off a **domino effect** that turned D-Mart into India's most successful retail chain.

√ **They raised ₹1,870 crore** from the IPO, giving them instant capital to expand aggressively.

√ **Their brand reputation exploded.** Suddenly, customers didn't just see them as a store—they saw them as a listed company they could trust.

√ **Their valuation skyrocketed.** Within one year, D-Mart's market cap doubled. Within three years, it was worth over ₹2 lakh crore.

√ **They became India's most profitable retail chain.** Unlike competitors drowning in debt, D-Mart had access to unlimited capital from public investors.

And today? **D-Mart is valued at over ₹2.5 lakh crore.**

One IPO. One decision. A chain reaction that changed the company's future forever.

IPO Domino #1: Your Brand Gets Instant Trust and Credibility

Before an IPO, you're just another private business. After an IPO, you're suddenly a **trusted, publicly listed company.**

What does that mean?

√ **Bigger clients take you seriously.** Imagine pitching your services to a large enterprise. If you're a private company, they might hesitate. But if you're listed? They see stability. They see transparency. They see a brand they can trust.

√ **Banks and financial institutions chase you.** Before an IPO, you're the one knocking on bank doors, struggling to secure funding. After an IPO, the same banks **start offering you better loan terms** because they see you as a low-risk, high-potential company.

√ **Investors line up to fund your next moves.** The moment you're on the stock market, people want to put money into your business. This means you **never have to worry about funding again.**

Think about it—what would change for your business if people instantly **trusted your brand**?

IPO Domino #2: Top Talent Wants to Work for You

If you want to build a billion-dollar company, you need **the best talent in your industry.** But here's the problem:

Top talent doesn't want to work for just any company.

They want:

√ Job security.

√ Career growth.

√ Equity in a growing business.

And guess what? **Public companies offer all three.**

√ Instead of paying **only** salaries, you can offer **ESOPs (Employee Stock Ownership Plans)**, just like Infosys, TCS, and Reliance.

√ You can attract **better leadership teams** because executives prefer working for listed companies with long-term stability.

√ You can compete with the biggest players for **top-tier employees.**

Let's look at the numbers.

Company	Employees Pre-IPO	Employees Post-IPO (5 Years Later)
D-Mart	5,000	12,000+
Zomato	3,000	6,500+
Nykaa	1,500	2,200+

An IPO doesn't just raise money—it makes you a **talent magnet.**

IPO Domino #3: Unlimited Capital for Future Growth

Here's a secret that private business owners don't know:

Once you go public, raising money is no longer a problem.

In a private company, if you need funds, you have to:

× Convince banks to lend you money.

× Convince investors to write a check.

× Burn through your savings.

But once you're listed, **raising capital is as simple as issuing more shares.**

√ Need ₹100 crore for expansion? Issue new shares.

√ Need to acquire a competitor? Use stock as a currency.

√   Want to expand into new markets? The market funds your growth.

You no longer have to **wait years** to generate profits for expansion. You can grow **instantly**—just like India's biggest companies have done.

IPO Domino #4: Your Valuation Skyrockets

Here's a simple formula:

The moment you go public, your company becomes worth more.

Why? Because the market decides your value—not just your annual profits.

- Before the D-Mart IPO, its **valuation was ₹2,000 crore.**
- One year after the IPO? **₹40,000 crore.**
- Today? **₹3 lakh crore.**

That's a **140X increase in valuation.**

What would happen if your business was valued 10X higher overnight?

√   You could attract **bigger investors.**

√   You could use your stock to **acquire competitors.**

√   You could leverage your higher valuation to **raise even more capital.**

And remember—**all of this started with just one IPO.**

IPO Domino #5: You Become a Market Leader Instead of a Follower

There are two types of businesses:

Followers – They grow slowly, take small risks, and struggle to scale.

Market Leaders – They dominate their industries with access to unlimited capital.

Going public **pushes you into the leader category.**

- **Private companies are reactive.** They wait, they hesitate, they play it safe.

- **Public companies are aggressive.** They expand fast, acquire competitors, and build industry dominance.

What kind of business do you want to run?

Checklist: The IPO Domino Effect – Is Your Business Ready?

√ **You want to raise capital without taking on debt.**

√ **You want to build a brand that people trust instantly.**

√ **You want to attract top talent and retain them with ESOPs.**

√ **You want to scale faster than your competitors.**

√ **You want unlimited access to future funding.**

The truth is, the **real benefits of an IPO aren't just financial— they're transformational.**

The moment you take this step, you **unlock an entirely new level of business growth.**

So, are you ready to set off the IPO Domino Effect?

Scan the QR Code → Answer a Few Simple Questions →

Get a Custom Eligibility Check Report from Our Expert Team.

CHAPTER - 6

THE PRE-IPO PLAYBOOK – WHAT YOU MUST FIX BEFORE GOING PUBLIC

Most Businesses Aren't IPO-Ready – Here's How to Fix That

Going public isn't just about listing your company on the stock exchange. **It's about proving to investors that your business is worth betting on.**

Many founders make a critical mistake: **They rush into an IPO without fixing the internal issues that could destroy their public market debut.**

√　**Weak financial records? Investors will run.**

√　**Messy corporate governance? SEBI will block you.**

√　**No scalable growth plan? Your IPO will flop post-listing.**

The **biggest IPO failures** didn't happen because of bad products or industries. **They happened because companies weren't IPO-ready.**

Before you even **think** about an IPO, **your business needs to meet these five critical IPO-readiness standards.**

Let's break them down.

1. **Financial Clean-Up – Your Numbers Must Be Investor-Ready**

Investors are **not** gamblers. **They won't put money into a company with shaky financials.** If your numbers aren't clean, **fix them NOW.**

What Investors Want to See:	What Kills an IPO:
√ Consistent revenue growth (at least 3 years of financial history).	√ Unstable earnings – Fluctuating revenue raises red flags.
√ Profitability (or a clear path to profitability).	√ High debt levels – Investors fear financial stress.
√ Minimal debt and strong cash flow.	√ Pending tax or legal issues – SEBI won't approve your IPO.
√ Audited financial statements—no "creative accounting."	

Action Steps:

→ Get your financials audited by a reputed firm.

→ Fix inconsistencies in revenue reporting.

→ Settle any outstanding debts or liabilities.

Case Study: Nykaa's Financial Fix Before IPO Before Nykaa went public in 2021, it spent **two years fixing financial leaks.** The company **restructured its business model** and ensured **consistent profitability before launching its IPO.**

The result? A **₹5,352 crore IPO and a ₹50,000 crore market cap.**

2. **Corporate Governance – Avoid the "Family Business" Trap**

   Public companies play by a different rulebook. **What worked in your privately held business won't fly in an IPO.**

√ **No more "one-man show" leadership.**

√ **No more vague accounting practices.**

√ **No more treating the company like a personal bank account.**

What You Need to Fix:

√ **Build a Strong Board of Directors.** Investors want **independent directors** who bring credibility—not just family members.

√ **Improve Internal Controls.** SEBI and investors **need transparency in financial decisions.**

√ **Separate Business from Personal.** No personal expenses disguised as "business costs."

Real-World Example: How Infosys Built Governance Before IPO

Infosys **didn't just scale operations**—it **built a strong governance structure.** By the time it launched its IPO in 1993, it had a **board of independent directors, transparent financials, and strict compliance policies.** Investors saw a **serious company—NOT a family-run business.**

3. **Business Scalability – Prove That You Can Grow**

   Going public isn't just about where your company is today. **It's about where it can go in the next 5-10 years.**

   Investors won't fund businesses that are "too small to scale."

   What Makes a Business Scalable?

√ **High customer demand with room for growth.**

√ **Expanding market opportunity.**

√ **Strong operational systems that can scale.**

√ **A leadership team with a clear vision for expansion.**

What Kills an IPO?

× Over-reliance on the founder. If the company falls apart without you, investors won't buy in.

× No clear expansion plan. A business with no roadmap beyond the IPO will struggle post-listing.

Action Steps:

→ Define your 5-year growth strategy. Investors want to know where the company is headed.

→ Automate and streamline operations so growth doesn't lead to chaos.

→ Build a strong leadership team that can scale the business without micromanagement.

4. **Competitive Advantage – Why Should Investors Choose YOU?**

    Investors don't just compare your company to other IPOs. **They compare it to every other investment opportunity available.**

    You need to **answer one BIG question: Why should investors buy YOUR stock instead of putting money into a more established company?**

    What Makes Investors Take You Seriously?

√ **Market leadership** – You're the top player in your niche.

√ **Differentiation** – Your business offers something competitors can't.

√ **Strong brand & customer loyalty.**

What Scares Investors Away?

× No real competitive edge. If your business can be easily copied, investors won't trust it.

× Weak branding. Unknown companies struggle to gain investor interest.

× Lack of market demand. If there's no clear reason for your growth, your IPO will flop.

Case Study: How D-Mart Used Competitive Advantage to Dominate

Before its IPO in 2017, **D-Mart wasn't India's biggest retailer.** But it had something more valuable—**an unbeatable pricing model that competitors couldn't match.** That **competitive advantage** made investors rush in, and today, D-Mart is worth ₹**2.5 lakh crore.**

5. **The IPO Story – Investors Buy the Vision, Not Just the Business**

The final piece of IPO readiness? **Your investor story.**

You're not just selling shares. **You're selling a vision.**

√ **Why should investors believe in your company's future?**

√ **Why is this the perfect time to go public?**

√ **What's the big picture of your industry's growth?**

What Separates Great IPOs from Failed Ones?

√ **A clear, compelling growth story that investors understand.**

√ **A well-structured pitch deck that communicates your vision.**

√ **Strong media & PR presence to create investor excitement.**

Case Study: How Zomato's IPO Story Created Massive Demand

Before Zomato's IPO, **they didn't just talk about food delivery.** They positioned themselves as **the future of India's food-tech industry.** They emphasized **data, AI-driven**

logistics, and expansion into grocery and cloud kitchens. That vision attracted over ₹9,375 crore in investments.

Final Thoughts: Are You IPO-Ready?

Most businesses **aren't ready for an IPO when they first consider it.**

That's okay—**but it means you have work to do.**

If you ignore these steps, your IPO will struggle.

If you fix them NOW, your IPO will be unstoppable.

Checklist: Is Your Business IPO-Ready?

√   Financials are audited and investor-ready.

√   Corporate governance is strong with independent directors.

√   The business has a clear expansion strategy.

√   Competitive advantage is clearly defined.

√   The IPO story is compelling and investor-friendly.

If you **checked all five boxes,** you're ready to move to the next step: **The IPO Execution Roadmap.**

Up next: **A complete breakdown of the IPO process—step by step.**

Exclusive Workshop: How IPOs Actually Work

PART 3:
THE ULTIMATE IPO BLUEPRINT

How to Take Your Business Public... Step by Step

Alright. You get it. An IPO is the ultimate growth hack. You've seen how it can **transform ordinary businesses into market giants.** You've seen why bank loans and VCs are **limiting your potential** instead of fueling your success.

But now, we're getting into the **real stuff.**

Because let's be honest—**most businesses fail at the IPO stage, not because they aren't good enough, but because they don't know HOW to do it right.**

√   They mess up valuation.

√   They pick the wrong Merchant Banker.

√   They don't structure their IPO correctly.

√   They screw up marketing, leaving investors uninterested.

√   They wait too long, missing the prime moment to go public.

And guess what happens?

They **flop.** Their shares underperform. Their company tanks before it even gets a chance to scale.

But that's **not going to be you.**

This section is your ultimate **step-by-step playbook**—the exact process that **smart businesses follow** to get their IPOs right, attract investors, and **watch their stock price explode post-listing.**

What's Coming Next?

You need a **clear strategy.** No guesswork. No relying on half-baked advice.

In the next two chapters, we're breaking down **the exact formula** for IPO success.

√ **The IPO Roadmap – 9 Steps to Going Public**

The **step-by-step process** from decision to execution.

- How to structure your IPO correctly from day one.
- The biggest mistakes businesses make—and how to avoid them.
- Why your Merchant Banker is the most important player in this game.

√ **Valuation Hacks – How to Price Your IPO for Maximum Gains**

- **Pricing your IPO** isn't about picking a random number—it's about strategy.
- Why **overpricing can kill your listing.**
- Why **underpricing leaves crores on the table.**
- How companies **manipulate valuations** to attract investors—and how you can do it **ethically** to your advantage.

The Harsh Reality of IPO Failures

You might be wondering, **"If IPOs are so powerful, why do some companies fail?"**

Because **they don't prepare.**

Look at some of India's worst IPO disasters:

- **Paytm (2021)** – Overhyped, overpriced, and **lost 60% of its value** in the first few months.

- **Jet Airways** – Went public, raised money, **but never fixed its internal financial mess.**

- **Reliance Power (2008)** – Launched as India's biggest IPO at the time… and then **crashed within days.**

These companies weren't bad businesses. But they **didn't get the IPO formula right.**

- They didn't price it right.

- They didn't convince the right investors.

- They didn't plan for post-IPO growth.

That's why this section is so important.

What You'll Get From This Section

By the time you finish these chapters, **you'll have the confidence and clarity** to execute your IPO plan with precision.

Most businesses wing it. **They pay the price.** You won't. **You'll do it right.**

Here's what you'll walk away with:

√ The **IPO roadmap** that breaks down the entire process—so you never feel lost.

√ The **exact questions** to ask your Merchant Banker to avoid costly mistakes.

√ The **right way to price your IPO**—so investors rush in, not run away.

√ A **fail-proof plan** to turn your IPO into long-term success.

Next Steps

Now, we roll into **the next 2 chapters.**

This is where **we break it all down.**

No jargon. No fluff. Just **clear, actionable steps.**

If you've made it this far, **you're already ahead of 99% of business owners.**

Now, let's make sure you don't just go public—**you dominate the market.**

Turn the page. Let's get started.

CHAPTER - 7

THE IPO ROADMAP...
9 STEPS TO GOING PUBLIC

No More Guesswork. Here's EXACTLY How You Take Your Business Public.

So, you've decided to go public. **Great decision.**

But let's get one thing straight—**this isn't just about listing your shares on the stock exchange.**

This is about **engineering your IPO for massive success.**

Because here's the truth: **A poorly executed IPO is WORSE than not going public at all.**

√   If you mess up the valuation, **investors won't buy in.**

√   If you pick the wrong Merchant Banker, **your IPO will sink before it even launches.**

√   If you don't market your IPO properly, **no one will care about your stock.**

That's why **we're doing this right.**

This chapter **walks you through the entire IPO process—step by step—so you don't just launch... you dominate.**

Step 1: Get Your Business IPO-Ready

An IPO isn't just about raising money. **It's about proving to the market that your business is worth investing in.**

Ask yourself:

√   Do you have a scalable business model?

√   Are your financials strong and transparent?

√   Do you have a clear plan for post-IPO growth?

Most businesses fail at this stage because they **rush into the IPO process without fixing internal issues.** Before you even THINK about listing, **get your house in order.**

Action Steps:

1.   Get your financials **audited by a top-tier firm.**

2.   Make sure your business has **at least 3 years of solid revenue growth.**

3.   Identify and fix any **red flags** that could scare investors away.

Step 2: Pick the Right Merchant Banker (This Will Make or Break Your IPO)

Think of your Merchant Banker as the **captain of your IPO ship.**

They **advise you, structure your IPO, handle the paperwork, and connect you with investors.**

Pick the wrong one? **Your IPO is dead before it even begins.**

What a GREAT Merchant Banker Does:

√   Ensures your IPO is priced right—so you raise maximum capital.

√   Helps you attract the right investors.

√   Makes sure your IPO complies with Stock Exchange regulations.

Case Study: When Infosys went public in 1993, they picked a **merchant banker who helped them raise ₹16+ crore—transforming them from a small IT company into an industry leader.**

Action Steps:

1.   Interview **at least 3-5 Merchant Bankers** before choosing one.

2.   Ask about **their track record with SME IPOs.**

3.   Ensure they have a strong **network of institutional investors.**

Step 3: Conduct Due Diligence (Fix Your Numbers NOW)

Investors **scrutinize every detail** before they buy into an IPO.

That means your **financials, business structure, compliance, and corporate governance must be rock solid.**

Common Mistakes That Kill IPOs:

×   Messy financial records (no investor trusts unclear numbers).

×   Pending legal issues (scares away investors instantly).

×   Overstating revenue projections (investors aren't fools).

Action Steps:

1.   Get a legal and financial **due diligence report.**

2.   Ensure your **corporate structure is IPO-friendly.**

3.   Clean up **any regulatory or legal risks** before filing.

Step 4: Decide Your IPO Structure & Price It Right

Not all IPOs are the same. You need to **pick the right structure** for your business.

Your IPO Can Be:

√ **Fresh Issue** – New shares are issued, and the money raised goes directly into expanding the business.

√ **Offer for Sale (OFS)** – Existing shareholders sell part of their stake. However, **OFS cannot be the entire IPO.** As per SEBI guidelines:

- **OFS must be at least 50% of the promoter's shareholding** OR **at least 20% of the total IPO issue size... whichever is lower.**

√ **Hybrid** – A combination of both, allowing businesses to raise capital while also providing an exit option for early investors or promoters.

Pricing Strategy:

Overpricing Your IPO? Investors won't buy. **Underpricing?** You leave crores on the table.

Solution? Price it at a **valuation that balances demand and profitability.**

Action Steps:

1. Conduct **market research** on how similar businesses were priced.

2. Work with **your Merchant Banker to find the sweet spot.**

3. Ensure your IPO valuation is **backed by solid growth projections.**

Step 5: Prepare Your DRHP (Draft Red Herring Prospectus)

This is **the official document that SEBI reviews before approving your IPO.**

What's in the DRHP?

√ Financial history

√ Future growth plans

√ Risk factors

√ Management structure

Action Steps:

1. Work with your legal and financial team to draft a **clear, investor-friendly DRHP.**

2. Submit it to **SEBI for approval.**

Step 6: The Roadshow – Pitching to Investors

This is where you **sell your IPO to investors.**

Institutional investors, fund managers, HNIs (High Net-Worth Individuals) — **this is who will buy the bulk of your shares.**

A weak roadshow = Low investor interest = **Disaster.**

Action Steps:

1. Prepare a **killer investor pitch deck.**

2. Attend **pre-IPO meetings** with potential investors.

3. Showcase **why your business is a strong bet.**

Step 7: Stock Exchange Approval & IPO Launch Date

Once Stock Exchange approves your DRHP, you get **the green light to launch.**

Now, **it's all about timing.**

√ Don't launch in a bad market.

√ Don't list when investor sentiment is low.

√ The best time is when market conditions favor growth stocks.

Action Steps:

1. Finalize **your launch date with your Merchant Banker.**
2. Ensure your IPO gets **maximum media coverage.**

Step 8: IPO Subscription – The Moment of Truth

Once the IPO is live, investors start **bidding for shares.** Your goal? **Get oversubscribed.**

An oversubscribed IPO = **Huge demand = Higher stock price post-listing.**

Action Steps:

1. Monitor investor interest daily.
2. Ensure all **marketing and PR efforts are at full scale.**

Step 9: The Listing Day – Making Stock Market History

The **final step.** Your shares officially start trading on the stock exchange.

This is **the moment every founder dreams of—the day your company's name flashes on the stock ticker, the bell rings, and your years of hard work finally pay off.**

The bell rings. Your IPO journey is complete. **Tapasya safal hui.** Your vision, persistence, and risk-taking have brought you to this moment.

But the real test begins now. Your IPO success is determined by how your stock performs on **Day 1.**

√ If demand is high, **your stock jumps in value.**

√ If demand is low, **it sinks below the issue price.**

Action Steps:

- Ensure **post-IPO PR campaigns** keep investor interest high.
- Track your **stock performance** and prepare for volatility.
- Focus on **long-term growth**—because IPO success isn't just about Day 1; it's about building lasting value.

You made it. **The bell has rung, but the real journey has just begun.**

Final Words: Your Blueprint for IPO Success

There you have it. **The exact steps to go public successfully.**

Most business owners mess this up because **they don't have a plan.**

Now, **you do.**

Checklist: Are You IPO-Ready?

√ Do you have **strong financials and growth plans?**

√ Have you **picked the right Merchant Banker?**

√ Is your **IPO pricing set for success?**

√ Are your **investor pitches airtight?**

√ Do you have a **post-IPO growth plan?**

If the answer is **YES,** then you're ready.

Next Up: Valuation Hacks – How to Price Your IPO for Maximum Gains

Now that you know **HOW to go public,** let's talk about **HOW MUCH your company should be worth.**

Because **if you price it wrong, everything else falls apart.** Turn the page. Let's get into it.

Get 1-on-1 IPO strategy advice on WhatsApp..

VALUATION HACKS – HOW TO PRICE YOUR IPO FOR MAXIMUM GAINS

Why IPO Valuation Is the Most Critical Step

You can follow every step of the IPO process perfectly. You can have a scalable business model, a great merchant banker, and an oversubscribed IPO.

But if you price your IPO wrong—**you will lose money.**

√ Overprice it? Investors won't buy, your IPO will flop, and your company's reputation will take a hit.

√ Underprice it? You'll leave crores on the table that should have gone into your business.

√ Price it just right? You maximize demand, boost stock price post-listing, and raise the capital you actually need.

This chapter is about **getting your valuation right**—so you don't get crushed on listing day.

Step 1: Understand What Determines IPO Valuation

IPO valuation isn't just about what YOU think your company is worth.

It's about what **the market** is willing to pay.

Here are the **key factors that determine your IPO price:**

Factor	Why It Matters
Revenue & Profitability	Investors want companies with **strong, growing revenue** and **clear profitability trends.**
Industry & Market Conditions	A **hot industry** can command **higher valuations.**
Competitive Position	If you're a **market leader**, your valuation goes up. If you're just another player, investors won't pay a premium.
Growth Potential	Investors care more about **future growth** than past performance.
Debt Levels	High debt? **Lower valuation.** Low debt? **Stronger financials = higher valuation.**
Investor Demand	The more investors want your shares, the higher your IPO can be priced.

Step 2: Choose the Right Valuation Method

There are **three main ways** to calculate your IPO price:

1. Price-to-Earnings (P/E) Ratio

√ The most common method.

√ Compares your company's stock price to its earnings per share (EPS).

√ Example: If your company has **₹10 crore in net profits** and a typical industry P/E ratio is **20X**, your valuation would be **₹200 crore.**

2. Discounted Cash Flow (DCF) Method

√   Best for companies with **strong future cash flow potential.**

√   Uses projected future earnings and discounts them to today's value.

√   More complex but helps justify a **higher valuation** if you have **big growth plans.**

3. Relative Valuation Method

√   Compares your company to **other recently listed IPOs in the same industry.**

√   If a similar company went public at a ₹500 crore valuation, **investors will expect your pricing to be in the same range.**

Most companies use a **mix of all three methods** to set their IPO price.

Step 3: Avoid the 3 Biggest IPO Valuation Mistakes

Many business owners **ruin their IPO** by making these mistakes:

Mistake #1: Overestimating Your Company's Value

Every founder thinks their company is worth more than it really is.

But if you overprice your IPO:

×   Investors won't buy.

×   Your IPO will be undersubscribed.

×   Your stock price will crash on listing day.

Case Study: Paytm's IPO Disaster

In 2021, Paytm launched India's biggest IPO—₹18,300 crore.

They **overpriced it** at ₹2,150 per share.

Result?

√   Investors didn't buy in.

√   The stock **crashed 27%** on listing day.

√   Over ₹1 lakh crore in market value was wiped out.

Lesson? **A bad IPO valuation can destroy wealth overnight.**

Mistake #2: Underpricing to Attract Investors

Some companies **set their IPO price too low** to guarantee demand. But this means you **leave crores on the table**—money that should have gone into scaling your business.

Company: TheGlobe.com (Internet startup)

IPO Date: November 13, 1998

IPO Price: $9 per share

Market Reaction:

- Stock soared to **$97** on the first trading day
- Closed at **$63** (a **1,000% increase**)

Financial Impact:

- Raised **$30 million** but significantly **underpriced shares**
- Analysts estimate **$200 million was left on the table—** capital that could have been used for growth

Lesson: Underpricing an IPO can lead to **short-term investor gains but long-term capital loss for the company**

Mistake #3: Ignoring Market Timing

The right IPO at the wrong time = **disaster.**

If the market is crashing or investors are risk-averse, **even a great company will struggle to raise funds.**

Case Study: Reliance Power's Overhyped IPO

Reliance Power launched its IPO in **2008—just before the global financial crisis.**

The company was strong, but **market conditions killed demand.**

√ The stock tanked **17% on listing day.**

√ Investors lost confidence.

√ It never recovered.

Lesson? **Market conditions matter as much as valuation.**

Step 4: Find the Sweet Spot for Your IPO Pricing

So, what's the right IPO price?

The answer:

√ High enough to raise maximum capital.

√ Low enough to **attract strong investor demand.**

Here's a **simple strategy** that works:

1. **Set a price band** (e.g., ₹250-₹275 per share).
2. **Test demand during the IPO roadshow.**
3. **Final price is based on investor appetite.**

If demand is **high**, you price at the top of the band. If demand is **weaker**, you go lower.

This ensures you **don't overprice or underprice**—you let the market decide.

Visualizing IPO Valuation Mistakes

1. Why Overpricing Kills IPOs

A simple chart comparing **overpriced vs. correctly priced IPOs** over time:

IPO Pricing	Investor Demand	Stock Performance (1 Year After Listing)
Overpriced	Low	Falls 20-50%
Fairly Priced	High	Gains 50-200%
Underpriced	Very High	Gains 200%+ (but company raises less capital)

2. The Impact of Market Timing on IPO Performance

A bar chart showing how **market conditions affect IPO success rates.**

Example: IPOs launched in **bull markets** vs. **bear markets.**

Market Condition	IPO Success Rate
Bull Market	85% IPOs oversubscribed
Stable Market	65% IPOs oversubscribed
Bear Market	30% IPOs oversubscribed

Final Thoughts: Your IPO Price = Your First Impression

Your IPO price isn't just about raising money.

It's **the first signal you send to the stock market.**

A well-priced IPO =

√   Strong investor confidence.

√   High demand.

√   A great start for long-term stock performance.

A poorly priced IPO =

×   Weak demand.

×   Negative media coverage.

×   A rocky start in the public market.

So, get your pricing right. **It will define your IPO success.**

Checklist: How to Make Sure Your IPO Is Priced to Win

√   Have you analyzed competitor IPOs and their pricing?

√   Are you using a **P/E ratio, DCF, and market comparables** to set valuation?

√   Have you tested pricing with investors before finalizing?

√   Are market conditions **favorable for your IPO launch?**

√   Is your price band **flexible** based on demand?

Exclusive Workshop: How IPOs Actually Work

CHAPTER - 9

THE IPO ADVISOR ADVANTAGE – HOW EXPERTS MAKE THE PROCESS EASY

Why Most Business Owners Feel Overwhelmed by the IPO Process

Let's be real—the idea of going public sounds exciting, but the actual process? That's where most business owners freeze.

And for good reason.

Taking your company public isn't just about raising money. It's about navigating a financial and regulatory maze filled with deadlines, documentation, compliance checks, and investor expectations. One misstep and you could end up in legal trouble, with a failed IPO, or worse—a stock price that crashes on listing day.

But here's the good news: **You don't have to do this alone.**

This is where an IPO advisor comes in. Think of them as your **IPO GPS** - guiding you through the process, avoiding the pitfalls, and ensuring that your public market debut is a massive success. Trying to DIY this? That's like performing your own brain surgery after watching a YouTube tutorial. **It won't work.**

What an IPO Advisor Actually Does (Beyond Just Paperwork)

A lot of business owners think an IPO advisor is just someone who fills out forms and makes sure the paperwork is in order. That's a **dangerous misconception.**

A good IPO advisor is not just a consultant—**he is the architect of your IPO.** The choices he helps you make can determine whether your IPO **thrives or struggles.** That's why choosing the right **intermediaries**—from anchor investors to underwriters— is as crucial as the decision to go public itself.

A Great IPO Advisor Helps You:

√ **Optimize Your IPO Timing**: Markets fluctuate. A great IPO advisor will analyze **market trends and investor sentiment** to ensure you list when demand is high, **maximizing valuation.**

√ **Set the Right Valuation**: Overprice your IPO, and investors stay away. Underprice it, and you leave money on the table. An advisor helps you **hit the sweet spot.**

√ **Structure Your IPO for Maximum Gains**: The right balance between **promoter holding, anchor investors, and retail allocation** can **make or break your IPO's success.**

√ **Choose the Right Intermediaries**: Your IPO success is not just about your business—it's about the **people handling your IPO.** The right **merchant bankers, anchor investors, underwriters, and legal advisors** play a massive role in ensuring a smooth listing. A strong advisor will help you **pick the best team** to guide your IPO journey.

√ **Navigate Regulatory Compliance**: SEBI, stock exchanges, auditors—there are multiple layers of compliance. A skilled

IPO advisor ensures that **everything meets the highest legal standards,** avoiding costly delays and regulatory hurdles.

√ **Manage Your Roadshow & Investor Pitching**: Getting the right investors on board is key. Advisors help you **create a compelling pitch, set up investor meetings, and generate market excitement** before listing day.

√ **Help Align Your Family with the IPO Vision**: If your family isn't on board, the IPO journey gets **ten times harder.** Advisors don't just help with financials; they help **explain the long-term benefits, reduce fear, and ensure your family sees this as a strategic, calculated move—not a reckless gamble.**

√ **Prepare for the Post-IPO Journey**: Listing is just the **beginning.** A strong advisor will help you **manage post-IPO expectations, stock performance, and investor relations.**

Bottom Line: Choose Wisely

Your IPO advisor is not just a guide—**he is the backbone of your IPO.** The right one **maximizes valuation, minimizes risks, and ensures a seamless listing.** Choose wrong, and you risk stumbling at every step. **Pick your IPO architect wisely.**

The Architect of Your IPO

An IPO is not just a financial transaction—it's the equivalent of **constructing a skyscraper.** You wouldn't break ground without an experienced architect, right? The same logic applies to your IPO.

A seasoned IPO advisor is **not just a GPS** helping you navigate the journey; they are the **lead architect** responsible for designing the entire foundation of your company's transition into the public market. Every single detail—**from valuation and regulatory**

compliance to investor confidence and market positioning—must be executed with precision.

Think of it this way:

- **A weak IPO structure?** That's like building a skyscraper without considering wind resistance—it will collapse under pressure.

- **A poorly timed launch?** That's like placing windows in a way that blocks sunlight—it diminishes the value of the final product.

- **An incorrect valuation?** That's like using the wrong materials—either overpriced and unaffordable, or undervalued and unsustainable.

A great IPO advisor ensures that your public listing stands tall, **attracting investors, maintaining market confidence, and sustaining long-term value.** Without the right architect, you risk structural weaknesses that could cause your IPO to **crumble before it even takes off.**

A key aspect of this architectural role is **investor storytelling—** crafting a compelling narrative that resonates with both institutional and retail investors. Advisors don't just focus on numbers; they position your business as an attractive long-term opportunity, making sure that investors buy into your vision, not just your stock.

How an Advisor Helps You Focus on Running and Scaling Your Business

Here's the harsh reality—many businesses that go public without proper guidance end up struggling **because the founder is too distracted** trying to manage the IPO process.

The entire journey takes months, sometimes years. If you try to handle everything yourself, it means **less focus on operations, sales, and customer experience**—the very things that make your business valuable in the first place.

An IPO advisor takes the burden off your shoulders. While you keep growing the business, they handle:

√ **Financial audits and due diligence**

√ **Drafting the Draft Red Herring Prospectus (DRHP)**

√ **Coordinating with merchant bankers and stock exchanges**

√ **Building an IPO marketing strategy**

√ **Ensuring SEBI compliance**

√ **Managing institutional investor relations**

√ **Helping you address family concerns and internal leadership alignment**

A great advisor doesn't just make the process smooth—they ensure you maximize every opportunity your IPO brings.

The Hidden Benefits of an IPO Advisor

Most business owners assume that an IPO advisor's job is limited to documentation, compliance, and handling legal formalities. But the best advisors bring so much more to the table—**they serve as strategists, risk mitigators, and success accelerators.**

Here's what **great** IPO advisors do that many don't realize:

√ **Crisis Management & Damage Control**: If a potential red flag arises—whether it's a compliance issue, investor hesitancy, or an external market fluctuation—seasoned advisors **step in immediately to mitigate the damage.** Without expert intervention, even a minor misstep can spiral into a PR disaster.

√ **Insider Market Knowledge & Timing Mastery**: IPO success is about more than just numbers—it's about understanding **market sentiment, investor psychology, and timing.** The right advisor **identifies the perfect launch window** to ensure your IPO receives maximum demand.

√ **Regulatory Advocacy**: A skilled IPO advisor doesn't just **comply with SEBI regulations**—they **proactively work with regulatory bodies** to **streamline approvals, anticipate challenges, and ensure a smooth listing.** They know how to structure an IPO in a way that meets all legal requirements while still maximizing value.

√ **Access to High-Value Investors**: Advisors with **deep industry connections** don't just help you attract funding; they introduce you to the **right** investors—ones who align with your long-term vision and add strategic value beyond just capital.

√ **Post-IPO Stability & Long-Term Growth Strategy**: Many businesses focus so much on getting listed that they neglect what happens **after** the IPO. Strong advisors prepare you for **post-IPO volatility, shareholder management, and sustaining long-term valuation growth.**

Bottom Line: If you think an IPO advisor is just about handling paperwork, you're **underestimating** the role they play. **They are your safeguard, your strategist, and your key to unlocking the full potential of your IPO.** Choosing the right one isn't just smart—it's essential for success.

The 5 Biggest IPO Mistakes Business Owners Make Without an Advisor

1. **Going Public at the Wrong Time**: Market sentiment matters. A bad launch window can kill investor enthusiasm.

2. **Overvaluing or Undervaluing the IPO**: If you don't get this right, you either struggle to get subscribers or leave crores on the table.

3. **Ignoring SEBI Compliance**: Small legal mistakes can delay or even cancel your IPO.

4. **Weak Investor Pitching**: Investors don't just look at financials; they need a compelling growth story.

5. **Failing to Plan Post-IPO Strategy**: Many businesses celebrate after listing, only to realize they have no plan for long-term shareholder value creation.

Thinking of doing this without an advisor? That's like stepping into the stock market without knowing how to read a balance sheet. You might get lucky, but chances are, you'll get crushed.

Real-World Case Study: How an IPO Advisor Helped Happiest Minds Technologies Succeed

Happiest Minds Technologies, a Bengaluru-based IT services company, went public in **September 2020**. While they had strong fundamentals and growth potential, they leveraged expert IPO advisory to ensure a smooth and highly successful listing.

What made their IPO a success?

- They worked closely with financial and legal advisors to ensure their **Draft Red Herring Prospectus (DRHP)** was flawless, **gaining SEBI clearance without delays.**

- Their IPO was **priced strategically** to appeal to both institutional and retail investors.

- They conducted **well-structured pre-IPO roadshows**, generating high investor interest.

- The result? The IPO was oversubscribed **151 times**, and the stock price surged **111% on listing day.**

Key Lesson:

- Happiest Minds didn't "wing it" or try to handle everything in-house. They brought in the right experts from day one. The result? A massively successful IPO that rewarded investors and positioned the company as a market leader.

Without an expert team guiding them, this kind of success wouldn't have been possible.

Checklist: What to Look for in an IPO Advisor

Not all advisors are created equal. Here's how to choose the right one:

√ **Proven Track Record** – Have they successfully handled IPOs similar to yours?

√ **Deep SEBI & Compliance Knowledge** – They should know the latest regulations inside out.

√ **Valuation Expertise** – Do they understand how to price your IPO optimally?

√ **Strong Investor Network** – Can they connect you with key institutional investors?

√ **Full-Process Support** – Do they only handle paperwork, or do they assist with strategy, roadshows, and post-IPO scaling?

Final Thoughts: The Right IPO Advisor is an Investment, Not an Expense

Some business owners hesitate to hire an IPO advisor, thinking it's an unnecessary cost. But the reality is **a single mistake in the IPO process can cost you crores**—way more than what you'd pay for expert guidance.

If you're serious about making your IPO a success, bringing in an expert isn't just smart—it's essential.

Next Steps: Want to see if your business is IPO-ready?

Get 1-on-1 IPO strategy advice on WhatsApp.

PART 4:
WHAT HAPPENS
AFTER YOUR IPO?

Scaling, Managing Shareholders, and Long-Term Success

Your IPO Was the Hard Part - Now Comes the Fun

Congratulations! You've gone public. Your company is now listed, investors have poured in money, and you've crossed the IPO finish line.

Take a moment to appreciate what you've just accomplished. This was the toughest part—navigating regulations, attracting investors, getting through the roadshows. **You've made it.**

Now, it's time to **fully enjoy the rewards** of being a public company.

Going public is like unlocking a cheat code for business growth. Suddenly, opportunities that once felt out of reach are now right in front of you:

- **Fueling Expansion on Your Terms** – No more relying on expensive loans or private investors. You now have public capital to scale, innovate, and move at lightning speed.

- **Becoming a Market Leader** – Public companies command more trust, attract bigger clients, and are seen as the real deal. You're now playing in the big leagues.

- **Attracting Top Talent Effortlessly** – The best minds want to work for a company with strong financial backing and stock incentives. Hiring just became easier.

- **Creating Generational Wealth** – Your shares are not just numbers; they are assets that can appreciate massively. This is your wealth-building machine.

What's Next? Growth, Leverage, and Market Domination

This next phase is all about **using your IPO to your advantage**. The smartest founders don't just sit back and watch stock prices—they use their company's public status as a weapon for expansion and influence.

Take companies like **TCS, Infosys, and Reliance Industries**. They didn't just stop after their IPOs—they used the momentum to expand aggressively, acquire competitors, and become dominant forces in their industries.

And this is exactly where **you're headed.**

This section will show you how to **stay in control, keep investors excited, and use your public company status as a launchpad for something even bigger.**

What You'll Learn in This Section

We're diving into the **most powerful post-IPO strategies** that will help you scale effortlessly:

√ **How to keep investors engaged** and position your company as an unstoppable force.

√ **What to do when stock prices fluctuate**—and how to use volatility to your advantage.

√ **The biggest mistakes founders make after going public** (and how to sidestep them effortlessly).

√   **How to leverage your stock as a tool for acquisitions, partnerships, and expansion.**

√   **How to maintain a balance between aggressive growth and stable stock performance.**

√   **The secrets of handling quarterly earnings calls like a pro—without the stress.**

√   **Why this is just the beginning of your journey to industry domination.**

Your IPO was the gateway. Now, it's time to use it to build something truly legendary. **Let's go.**

CHAPTER - 10

LIFE AFTER THE IPO – MANAGING PUBLIC MARKET EXPECTATIONS

The Post-IPO Playbook: What Changes After You Go Public

You did it. Your company is now a publicly traded entity, your IPO was a success, and you have capital at your disposal. **Now, you have the power to scale bigger and faster than ever before.**

But while the IPO was a major milestone, **it's just the beginning of your company's next phase of growth**. The shift from a private company to a public one brings exciting opportunities, but it also comes with new responsibilities. The key to thriving post-IPO isn't just about managing stock prices—it's about positioning your company as an industry leader.

Your post-IPO journey will be defined by **momentum**. Companies that understand how to leverage their public status experience **explosive growth**—not just in stock value but in brand trust, market dominance, and strategic expansion.

So, what changes now that you're public?

√ **Increased Visibility & Credibility**: Your company is now on the radar of institutional investors, analysts, and media. This attention can fuel your growth if you manage it well.

√ **Access to More Capital**: Beyond the IPO, you can raise additional funds through follow-on offerings, bonds, and strategic partnerships.

√ **Stronger Hiring Power**: A public company with stock options attracts top-tier talent, allowing you to build an A-list team.

√ **Bigger Deals & Partnerships**: Your newfound credibility makes acquisitions, joint ventures, and expansion into new markets easier than ever.

The bottom line? **Going public is a power move—but only if you know how to play the game right.** Let's break down the most important things you need to focus on now.

The Importance of Investor Relations – Keeping Your Shareholders Happy

When you were private, you only had to answer to a handful of investors—maybe just yourself and a few close partners. **Now, you have thousands, even millions, of shareholders who expect transparency, growth, and returns.**

Winning in the post-IPO world is all about **investor confidence**. When shareholders trust you, they buy more, hold longer, and spread positive sentiment in the market. When trust is lost, stock prices tumble.

How to Build a Strong Investor Relations Strategy

Investor relations isn't just about issuing reports—it's about storytelling. The best companies don't just throw numbers at investors; they craft a compelling vision that excites and reassures shareholders. Take every earnings call, shareholder meeting, and media interview as an opportunity to reinforce your company's mission and roadmap.

A few key principles to follow:

1. **Communicate Your Vision Clearly**: Investors don't just buy stocks; they buy into a company's long-term vision. Keep them engaged with regular updates on your expansion plans, revenue streams, and innovation strategies.

2. **Master Half Yearly Earnings Calls**: This is your chance to showcase results, share insights, and maintain control over your company's narrative. Confident, clear, and data-backed presentations win investors over.

3. **Proactive Transparency**: Don't wait for problems to arise before addressing them. When investors feel like they're in the loop, they stay loyal–even in times of volatility.

4. **Attract the Right Investors**: Smart companies actively court long-term institutional investors who believe in their mission, rather than short-term traders who only care about quick profits.

Successful investor relations is about more than just satisfying financial analysts—it's about creating a movement around your stock. The more confidence you instill, the more valuable your company becomes.

Managing Stock Volatility – What to Do When Prices Fluctuate

Stock prices move—it's just part of the game. The key isn't to panic, but to **stay strategic**.

Think of stock volatility like ocean waves. A seasoned sailor doesn't fight the waves—they ride them. Your job as a public company leader is to **use stock price movements to your advantage**, rather than getting swept away by short-term fluctuations.

Three critical steps:

Step 1: Stick to the Fundamentals – Don't let daily price movements dictate your business strategy. Keep delivering strong results, and the stock will take care of itself.

Step 2: Control the Narrative – Proactively communicate during downturns. Investors will forgive temporary dips if they see a clear growth plan.

Step 3: Use Buybacks to Stabilize Prices – If the stock dips below fair value, repurchasing shares can reinforce investor confidence and signal strength.

Many of the world's most successful public companies have experienced temporary stock downturns—only to emerge stronger because they stuck to a clear, long-term strategy. The market will reward execution and confidence, so stay the course.

The 3 Biggest Mistakes Founders Make Post-IPO (And How to Avoid Them)

Many companies go public only to **struggle or stagnate** because they fail to adjust to their new reality. Here are the three biggest mistakes you MUST avoid:

Mistake #1: Losing Focus on Growth

Some founders get caught up in stock price performance instead of focusing on **scaling the business**. Growth is what keeps investors engaged—**stay aggressive, expand strategically, and keep the momentum going.**

Mistake #2: Poor Investor Communication

Silence kills confidence. If investors don't hear from you, they assume the worst. **Regular updates, transparent reports, and a clear vision** are the antidote to panic selling.

Mistake #3: Mishandling Stock Dilution

Issuing too many new shares without a strong reason weakens investor confidence. **Only raise more capital when you have a clear, high-value use case for it.**

Real-World Case Study: The Journey of Avenue Supermarts (D-Mart) Post-IPO

Avenue Supermarts, the parent company of **D-Mart**, is a **perfect example of how to handle life after an IPO the right way.**

When D-Mart went public in 2017, it had a strong reputation but was still seen as a regional player. Many doubted whether it could compete with larger, well-funded retail chains. However, **instead of focusing on stock price fluctuations, the company doubled down on execution.**

√ **They expanded strategically,** choosing store locations based on long-term profitability rather than short-term market pressure.

√ **They managed investor expectations effectively,** maintaining transparency and delivering consistent financial growth.

√ **They avoided reckless expansion,** ensuring that every new store was profitable rather than just growing for the sake of it.

√ **They used their IPO capital wisely,** strengthening their supply chain and maintaining cost efficiency.

The result? D-Mart's stock **skyrocketed over 1,000%** within five years of listing, proving that a disciplined post-IPO strategy is the key to long-term success.

Checklist: Running a Successful Public Company

Every successful public company follows a playbook. Here's how you ensure sustained success post-IPO:

√ **Investor Relations Must Be Proactive** – Shareholders should never feel like they're in the dark.

√ **Growth Comes First** – Keep your business moving forward, no matter what.

√ **Manage Stock Wisely** – Buybacks, strategic share issuance, and investor alignment matter.

√ **Capitalize on New Market Opportunities** – Use your IPO capital for intelligent expansion.

√ **Master Earnings Calls & Media** – Every message you send shapes market perception.

Running a successful public company isn't just about financials—it's about leadership, vision, and strategic decision-making.

Final Thoughts

You've already done the hard part—going public. Now, it's time to enjoy the benefits.

Your stock is more than just a market asset—it's a weapon for growth.

Handled correctly, your IPO will be the gift that keeps on giving—fueling expansion, driving influence, and cementing your company's place as an industry leader.

Now, let's take this a step further. In the next chapter, we'll explore how you can **leverage your stock to make billion-dollar moves**—from acquisitions to market expansion.

The game has changed. And you're in control.

Exclusive Workshop: How IPOs Actually Work

CHAPTER - 11

LEVERAGING YOUR IPO FOR BIGGER BUSINESS MOVES

Your IPO Was Just the Beginning—Now It's Time to Play the Big Game

Going public is **not the finish line—it's the start of a whole new playing field** where the stakes (and rewards) are much higher.

The best founders don't stop at raising capital; they **turn their IPO into a weapon for long-term dominance.**

This is where you shift from being a great business to **becoming an empire.**

Think of this as the moment when Amazon expanded beyond books, Tesla went from electric cars to energy solutions, and Reliance moved from petrochemicals to telecom and retail.

Your IPO has given you three things:

→ **Credibility:** Investors and the market take you seriously.

→ **Capital:** A war chest to fund your most ambitious moves.

→ **Stock Power:** Your shares are now an asset that can be used strategically.

So what do you do with this power? **You expand, acquire, and take control.**

This chapter is all about leveraging your IPO **to grow in ways that were impossible before.**

Your Stock is More Than Just a Share Price – It's a Weapon for Expansion

Your stock is no longer just a piece of paper—it's an asset that can be used to **finance growth without draining cash.**

Public companies don't just acquire competitors—they **swallow them whole** using stock-based deals.

- **Facebook bought WhatsApp for $19 billion—most of it in stock.**

- **Tesla acquired SolarCity in an all-stock transaction to dominate renewable energy.**

- **Tata Group used share swaps to merge key businesses and create massive conglomerates.**

Your stock is a bargaining chip. If a private company wants to sell, they no longer need to demand cash—you can offer equity instead.

This means you can **buy, expand, and grow exponentially— without ever touching your bank balance.**

How to Use Your Stock for Takeovers & Acquisitions

√ **Identify Your Targets** – Find smaller, undervalued competitors who add strategic value.

√ **Structure Stock Deals Smartly** – Avoid over-dilution by keeping share-based acquisitions within a calculated range.

√ **Pitch the Future** – If you're acquiring a company, the founders need to believe in your stock's future value.

√ **Use Mergers to Build an Ecosystem** – Don't just acquire companies—integrate them into a bigger vision.

IPO Capital is Not Just for Growth — It's for Achieving Market Leadership

Expansion doesn't just mean opening new offices or launching products—it means **becoming the dominant force in your industry.**

Case Study: How Reliance Used IPO Capital to Dominate Indian Retail & Telecom

Reliance didn't just expand after its IPO—it **fundamentally reshaped India's business landscape.**

- **They launched Jio**, disrupting telecom by making internet access nearly free.
- **They used IPO funding to invest in retail, eventually acquiring Future Group.**
- **They leveraged their stock to create Reliance Digital, taking on Amazon and Flipkart.**

Reliance didn't just compete. **They changed the game and forced others to follow their rules.**

Your IPO Playbook for Total Market Domination

Expand Where Others Can't – Use your IPO capital to enter new markets before competitors can afford to.

Make the Industry Rely on You – Invest in infrastructure, patents, or platforms that make others dependent on your company.

Acquire, Merge, and Consolidate – Buy out smaller players before they become threats.

Turn Your Stock Into a Fortress – The stronger your stock, the easier it becomes to raise capital and make moves that others can't.

Landing Billion-Dollar Deals – The Public Company Advantage

The real game begins **after you've built dominance**—when global investors, governments, and Fortune 500 companies start seeing you as a serious player.

Why Being Public Attracts Billion-Dollar Partnerships

- **Public companies attract institutional investors** who bring not just money, but connections and influence.
- **Big brands prefer working with listed companies** because transparency is higher.
- **Stock-backed deals make negotiations easier** because everyone has an exit strategy.

Case Study: Zomato's Billion-Dollar Play

Zomato's IPO wasn't just about raising money—it was about creating an empire.

- **They acquired Blinkit (formerly Grofers) in a stock-based deal** to enter the quick-commerce space.
- **Institutional investors jumped in post-IPO**, giving them long-term financial backing.
- **They used their public status to position themselves as India's dominant food-tech player.**

Had they stayed private, **none of this would have been possible at the same scale.**

Checklist: How to Go from IPO Success to Market

Domination

To truly **leverage your IPO**, your strategy needs to go beyond basic expansion. Here's how you **play the big game:**

√ **Use Your Stock Like Cash** – Make acquisitions without touching your bank balance.

√ **Plan Aggressive Market Takeovers** – Expand where your competitors are weakest.

√ **Structure Deals with Long-Term Impact** – Focus on stock-backed acquisitions and strategic partnerships.

√ **Position Yourself for Institutional Investment** – These are the players who bring billion-dollar funding.

√ **Think 10 Years Ahead** – Every move should build toward your ultimate market dominance.

Final Thoughts

The companies that dominate after going public aren't just focused on growth—they're focused on total market control.

Your IPO has **given you the resources, credibility, and leverage to play at the highest level.**

Now, the question isn't just **how big you can grow—but how big you can win.**

What's your next move?

Get 1-on-1 IPO strategy advice on WhatsApp.

PART 5:
THE IPO EFFECT - HOW IT TRANSFORMS YOUR BUSINESS & FUTURE

The IPO: More Than Just Money

By now, you've understood the fundamentals of IPOs—what they are, how they work, and the mindset shift required to take your company public. You've seen how successful businesses use IPOs as a launchpad, not just for raising funds, but for creating long-term wealth, influence, and exponential growth.

But here's the part no one talks about enough: **Going public doesn't just change your business—it transforms everything.**

The Perception Shift: How the Market Sees You Differently

An IPO isn't just about financial capital; it's about unlocking new possibilities that were never within reach before. Your company enters an entirely new playing field, where investors, partners, customers, and even your own employees begin to see you differently. **The way the world interacts with your business shifts.** The authority and credibility of a publicly traded company often open doors to partnerships and opportunities that were previously inaccessible. Whether it's securing better terms with vendors, attracting higher-caliber talent, or drawing the attention of global investors, the benefits extend far beyond the balance sheet.

Leveling Up: The IPO as a Business Accelerator

Moreover, the IPO process forces business owners to level up. The scrutiny, compliance, and operational discipline required to go public make your company stronger, more structured, and primed for sustainable success. Suddenly, you're not just running a business—you're leading a publicly accountable entity, and that changes the way you approach everything from decision-making to long-term strategy.

The Hidden Benefits of IPOs

In this section, we're diving into the **six major benefits** that an IPO brings—benefits that most entrepreneurs don't even realize until they experience them firsthand. From attracting mentorship and manifesting success, to skyrocketing your company's valuation and automating your business for scale, these are the hidden superpowers of going public.

You'll also discover how companies that embrace these changes thrive while others struggle. The difference lies in mindset, adaptability, and leveraging the full spectrum of advantages that come with an IPO. Public companies that understand this not only survive but dominate their industries, outpacing competitors and cementing their market position for decades to come.

Here's what you'll discover in this Part:

1. **The IPO Manifestation Effect:** How shareholders, investors, and market forces begin manifesting success alongside you.

2. **The Free Mentorship Hack:** Why major investors become your biggest advisors—without charging a fee.

3. **The Mindset Shift:** How an IPO Transforms Wealth and Business Growth.

4. **The Sales & Reputation Engine:** How IPOs bring free marketing, top-tier vendors, and world-class talent.

5. **The IPO Wealth Formula:** Using IPO funds to reduce debt, stabilize cash flow, and fuel expansion.

6. **Scaling Smart:** Why IPOs give you the financial muscle to automate and future-proof your business.

Going public is just the beginning. Now, let's explore how it changes the game forever.

CHAPTER - 12

THE IPO MANIFESTATION EFFECT - WHEN THE MARKET PRAYS FOR YOUR SUCCESS

The Power of Collective Manifestation

Before an IPO, your business's success depends entirely on you and your internal team. You're the one envisioning growth, pushing forward, and making things happen. But once you go public, something fundamental shifts: **you're no longer the only one manifesting success.**

Every investor who buys into your company is betting on your future. They want you to win just as much as you do—because when your stock price rises, so does their wealth. Suddenly, your business becomes a collective vision, driven by thousands of people who believe in your potential. **The more people who believe in you, the stronger your business's momentum becomes.**

From Solo Dream to Shared Reality

Think of it like this: when you're a private business owner, you're building a house alone. Every brick, every nail—it's on you. But when you go public, thousands of people start helping you build that house, investing their time, money, and belief into making it bigger, stronger, and more valuable. The weight of success no longer sits solely on your shoulders—it's distributed among a network of shareholders, stakeholders, and market forces all rooting for you.

This shift doesn't just reduce the burden—it amplifies your capacity to dream bigger. With collective backing, you now have the potential to scale faster, attract top-tier partnerships, and enter new markets that once seemed out of reach. Your business's reputation skyrockets because public perception shifts in your favor, bringing opportunities that wouldn't have been possible before.

Why Shareholder Energy Matters

Beyond financial investment, there's a psychological power in having an army of people wanting you to succeed. This kind of collective belief creates momentum. Media starts paying attention.

Customers see your brand differently. Potential partners take you more seriously. Your company's story gets amplified, and in turn, **that belief starts shaping reality**. It's not just optimism—it's a market force that drives demand, stock price, and long-term growth.

Shareholders also act as unofficial ambassadors for your brand. They talk about your company, defend it against skeptics, and advocate for its future success. This organic word-of-mouth marketing is **priceless**. When thousands of people have a vested interest in your success, they naturally spread the message further than any paid campaign ever could.

How to Leverage the IPO Manifestation Effect

Going public gives you the opportunity to harness this collective energy in powerful ways:

1. **Transparency Builds Trust**: Shareholders thrive on updates and transparency. The more they feel involved, the more invested they become—not just financially, but emotionally. Regular communication strengthens loyalty and keeps the momentum going.

2. **Momentum Drives Growth**: Excitement fuels market confidence. An engaged investor base means increased media coverage, higher public interest, and a stronger company reputation. Public enthusiasm can lead to stock price appreciation, allowing your company to raise more capital in future rounds.

3. **Your Vision Becomes Their Mission**: When shareholders believe in your company's future, they advocate for it. They spread the word, attract new investors, and even influence customer behavior in your favor. Their belief fuels demand, making your brand stronger and more desirable.

4. **The Fear of Missing Out (FOMO) Effect**: When early investors believe in your vision and start seeing results, others don't want to miss out. This creates a snowball effect, leading to even greater market attention and increased investments.

5. **Investor-Led Innovations**: Public companies often get feedback and insights from shareholders who have industry expertise. Some investors actively contribute ideas, connect you with potential partners, or push for innovations that elevate your company's growth trajectory.

The Bigger Picture

IPO success isn't just about raising funds—it's about igniting belief. The more people who want your business to succeed, the more likely it is to happen. This is why some companies explode in valuation post-IPO while others stagnate—the companies that actively harness shareholder energy thrive.

The biggest mistake entrepreneurs make post-IPO? **Ignoring their investors.** Companies that treat shareholders as partners rather than just financial contributors create a powerful network of advocates who are emotionally and financially invested in the company's future.

If you embrace this mindset, the IPO becomes more than just a liquidity event—it transforms into a long-term force multiplier for your brand and business.

In the next chapter, we'll discuss another hidden perk of going public: **how big investors become your personal mentors - without charging you a single rupee.**

CHAPTER - 13

THE FREE MENTORSHIP HACK - HOW BIG INVESTORS GUIDE YOU TO THE TOP

Why Investors Make the Best Mentors

When you were running a private business, getting top-tier mentorship wasn't easy. Most successful business leaders don't have the time to coach others, and hiring high-level advisors costs a fortune. But something **magical** happens when you go public—mentorship finds you.

Big investors don't just put money into your stock. They put in their time, their insights, and their connections. Why? Because your success is now directly tied to their wealth. When your company grows, their investments multiply. That's why the smartest investors don't just buy and hold—they help steer the ship. And unlike paid mentors, these investors **want you to win for their own benefit**.

How an IPO Attracts Power Players

Once your company is listed, it starts attracting high-net-worth individuals, institutional investors, and market veterans. These are people who have decades of experience in scaling businesses, navigating market cycles, and making strategic decisions that drive massive success. And here's the best part—they now have a **vested interest** in making sure you don't fail.

This means that when you need guidance, you no longer have to pay for expensive consultants or struggle to get on the radar of industry leaders. Instead, major investors will **proactively** reach out, offering advice, introductions, and strategic direction—often without you even asking.

Shark Tank India & The Real Motive Behind Investment Pitches

If you've watched **Shark Tank India**, you'll notice something interesting: not every entrepreneur who pitches their business is actually looking for money. Many of them are after something much more valuable—**mentorship.** They know that getting a Shark as an investor isn't just about securing funds; it's about gaining access to their expertise, network, and business acumen.

When a startup lands an investment from someone like **Aman Gupta (boAt), Peyush Bansal (Lenskart), or Anupam Mittal (Shaadi.com)**, they don't just get capital. They get **a seat at the table with a high-level mentor** who has already navigated the journey they're about to embark on. This is the hidden advantage of investor relationships, whether through a TV show or in the real world of IPOs.

The same logic applies to **public companies**. Once you go public, your stock attracts seasoned investors who have built and scaled multi-million-dollar businesses. And just like the entrepreneurs on Shark Tank, your goal should be to leverage their experience, not just their money.

The Hidden Perks of Investor Mentorship

1. **Exclusive Industry Insights**: The investors who back your company aren't just throwing money around. They have experience across industries, trends, and business cycles that you can tap into.

2. **Unmatched Network Access**: Investors want to see you scale, so they open doors to potential partners, clients, and even government connections that would otherwise take years to establish.

3. **Crisis Management & Strategy**: When challenges arise, seasoned investors can guide you through downturns, market fluctuations, and unexpected disruptions with tried-and-tested strategies.

4. **Investor-Led Innovation**: Many investors have insights into emerging trends and technologies that they share with you, helping your company stay ahead of the curve.

5. **Instant Credibility & Trust**: Just like Shark Tank investors boost the credibility of startups, having the backing of respected market players gives your company an instant reputation boost.

The Bigger Picture

Your IPO doesn't just raise money—it brings a level of strategic mentorship that private businesses rarely get access to. Investors don't just believe in your business; they **become part of its success story.**

If you know how to nurture these relationships, your investors can become the **most valuable mentors and allies you'll ever have.**

In the next chapter, we'll discuss the biggest mental shift that happens post-IPO—how your focus moves from profits to valuation and why that's the key to real wealth.

CHAPTER - 14

THE MINDSET SHIFT: FROM PROFITS TO VALUATION

The Old Game vs. The New Game

Before an IPO, business owners are laser-focused on one thing: **profitability.** Every decision is measured by its immediate impact on revenue and net earnings. That's the game when you run a private company—you need to make money, stay cash-flow positive, and keep operations lean.

But the second you go public, **the game changes.** Now, it's no longer just about how much profit you make—it's about how much your company is **worth.** Valuation becomes the metric that drives decision-making, investor confidence, and long-term success. The smartest founders understand this shift and embrace it. Those who don't? They get left behind.

Old Game (Private Company Focus)	New Game (Public Company Focus)
× Profitability is the primary goal	√ Valuation and growth potential matter more

✗ Extract cash for owners & stakeholders	√ Reinvest earnings into expansion & innovation
✗ Avoid debt to maintain profitability	√ Use debt strategically to scale faster
✗ Focus on immediate revenue growth	√ Focus on long-term market dominance
✗ Limited to private investors	√ Open access to global capital markets
✗ Limited media attention & credibility	√ Higher visibility, credibility, and brand power
✗ Decisions based on short-term gains	√ Strategy aligned with future market position
✗ Controlled by a few stakeholders	√ Influenced by public sentiment & investor confidence

Why Valuation Matters More Than Profit

Look at some of the biggest companies in the world—Amazon, Tesla, Paytm, Zomato. For years, they weren't highly profitable, yet their valuations skyrocketed. Why? Because the market values **growth, future potential, and scalability** more than short-term earnings.

Here's the brutal truth: If you're still running your public company like a private business—obsessed with daily profits instead of big-picture expansion—you're playing the wrong game. Public markets reward companies that can demonstrate **growth potential, strategic investments, and a roadmap for dominance.**

The Key Shifts You Need to Make

1. **Reinvest, Don't Just Extract**: Private companies often pull out profits for owners and stakeholders. Public companies reinvest earnings into expansion, R&D, acquisitions, and market capture.

2. **Think in Market Caps, Not Monthly Margins**: Your stock price is a reflection of investor confidence. If you focus on driving valuation up, you create wealth far beyond what pure profits can generate.

3. **Leverage Debt & Capital Smartly**: While private businesses avoid debt to maintain profitability, public companies use debt strategically to scale faster and increase valuation.

4. **Investor Confidence is Everything**: Your valuation depends on how much the market believes in your company's future, not just its past performance.

5. **Long-Term Vision Over Quick Wins**: Businesses that focus on **disruptive innovation, global expansion, and strategic partnerships** see sustained valuation growth. Short-term profits are temporary, but a dominant market position is an asset that appreciates over time.

The Billion-Dollar Perspective

When Jeff Bezos ran Amazon in the early years, he famously ignored calls for profitability. Instead, he poured money into customer experience, logistics, and scale. Investors backed him because they saw the bigger vision. Today, Amazon's valuation is astronomical—not because of early profits, but because Bezos played the long game.

The same is true for Indian companies. Flipkart ran at losses for years before Walmart acquired it for **$16 billion.** By focusing on growth and market dominance instead of short-term profits, they built an empire that attracted massive valuation.

Startups that aim to scale rapidly and establish a monopoly often see greater investor interest than those simply trying to maintain small, steady profits. Market leaders aren't necessarily the ones who made the most money in their first few years—they're the ones who positioned themselves for long-term success.

Common Pitfalls Founders Must Avoid

Transitioning from a private mindset to a public mindset isn't easy. Many founders make critical mistakes that **hurt** their valuation:

- **Over-Focusing on Quarterly Profits** – Public companies must balance short-term performance with long-term strategy. Short-term thinking kills future valuation.

- **Ignoring Market Sentiment** – Your valuation isn't just about numbers. Investor confidence, public perception, and brand narrative all play a role.

- **Underestimating the Power of Expansion** – Companies that aggressively expand post-IPO tend to see higher valuations than those that remain stagnant.

- **Failing to Communicate Vision to Investors** – The best CEOs sell a **story**—not just a balance sheet. Investors need a reason to believe in your company's long-term potential.

- **Fear of Taking Bold Moves** – Many companies play it safe post-IPO, fearing scrutiny. However, IPOs are about scale, and the ones that dominate markets take aggressive steps forward.

Why This Shift Is Non-Negotiable

If you want to truly leverage your IPO, you must **stop obsessing**

over short-term profits and start playing for market dominance. The businesses that thrive post-IPO are those that scale aggressively, reinvest strategically, and control the narrative around their valuation.

This shift requires **bold decision-making, relentless reinvestment, and a vision that extends far beyond quarterly profits.** Companies that recognize this become industry leaders—those that don't get lost in the crowd.

In the next chapter, we'll break down another powerful advantage of IPOs—how they turn your business into a sales and reputation powerhouse.

CHAPTER - 15

THE SALES & REPUTATION ENGINE - HOW AN IPO SUPERCHARGES YOUR BUSINESS

Why IPOs Are More Than Just Money

Many founders think of IPOs as a tool to raise funds. While that's true, the **real, long-term value of an IPO isn't just the money— it's the credibility, visibility, and brand power that comes with being a publicly listed company.**

An IPO instantly puts your business in the **spotlight.** Suddenly, you're no longer just another private company fighting for attention. The **market watches you, the media covers you, and your credibility skyrockets overnight.** This shift opens doors that were previously shut—whether it's attracting **premium clients, landing bigger deals, or forming partnerships** with top-tier vendors.

The Public Company Perception Advantage

Perception is everything in business. A private company, no matter how successful, still carries a level of uncertainty. But once you go public, everything changes. Customers, vendors, and partners **trust public companies more** because they operate under **strict regulations, financial transparency, and governance.** Media exposure also increases dramatically, as **business media actively follows IPOs** and public companies, giving you **free PR** that's hard to buy.

Large corporations prefer working with public companies because they view them as **more stable and long-term partners,** and top professionals are naturally drawn to brands that are seen as **industry leaders.** Having **institutional investors and retail shareholders** builds further **credibility,** making your company **more stable and respected** in the market. A **public listing separates you from private competitors,** giving you an **edge in negotiations and market positioning.**

How an IPO Fuels Sales Growth

Going public doesn't just give you a higher valuation—it gives you the **ultimate sales weapon: legitimacy and influence.** Many companies struggle with sales because they **lack market trust.** But after an IPO, your **brand gains authority,** and customers and businesses naturally gravitate toward **industry leaders.** Enterprise clients take you **more seriously** because many large corporations **only work with public companies** due to compliance and credibility factors.

A **high market cap signals strength,** making your company **more desirable** to potential buyers and partners. **Institutional investors and retail shareholders want your company to succeed,** which creates **organic word-of-mouth growth.** Additionally, **public companies are often favored** in government contracts and high-level business opportunities, giving you an **edge in securing lucrative deals.**

Vendor & Supplier Benefits: Why The Best Want to Work With You

Public companies get access to **better deals, better contracts, and better partnerships.** Vendors and suppliers see a public company as a **prestigious, long-term partner.** They know you have **capital, governance, and accountability,** which means **fewer risks** for them. Vendors **extend better credit terms** to public companies due to **financial transparency,** making cash flow management easier.

Being **publicly traded makes you an attractive partner** for **premium vendors and suppliers,** opening up **exclusive opportunities.** When vendors **know your brand is publicly recognized,** they are **more willing to negotiate** in your favor, giving you **stronger leverage.** Public companies with **high credibility get access to lower-cost goods and services,** allowing them to maintain **competitive pricing.** Many **multinational vendors prioritize public companies** for **international partnerships and expansions,** giving you **access to global supply chains** that can help fuel **large-scale growth.**

The Snowball Effect of Reputation & Growth

Once an IPO **boosts your credibility,** that trust **compounds over time.** Every **successful partnership, big deal, and media feature** adds another **layer of legitimacy** to your brand. This creates a **snowball effect,** where:

- **More businesses want to collaborate with you.**
- **Bigger clients start knocking at your door.**
- **Your stock price increases due to rising market confidence.**

- **Competitors struggle to match your level of trust and brand perception.**

- **Companies with strong public reputations find it easier to acquire or merge with others, further accelerating expansion and market dominance.**

Leveraging Your IPO for Maximum Business Growth

Going public isn't just about raising capital—it's about strategically using your **newfound credibility to unlock bigger opportunities.** Position yourself as a **market leader** by using your **IPO status** to dominate conversations in your industry. **Make strategic PR moves** by getting featured in **major business publications** to strengthen brand perception. **Showcase your IPO success** in sales pitches, using it as **proof of stability and long-term vision** to close big deals.

Public companies naturally get more media coverage— ensure you're **controlling the narrative** in a way that supports your **long-term growth.** Additionally, **developing an investor relations strategy** will **keep shareholders engaged** and maintain **long-term confidence** in your company, which is **crucial for sustaining valuation growth and business momentum.**

Why Your IPO Is a Sales & Reputation Game-Changer

Going public turns your company into an **industry powerhouse.** You gain not only **capital but also influence, trust, and long-term business momentum.**

Public perception is **one of the biggest assets** a company gains post-IPO. If leveraged correctly, it can fuel **unstoppable growth, better partnerships, and industry dominance.**

A **well-managed public image,** combined with **strategic PR and investor engagement,** ensures that your company remains a **market leader long after the IPO buzz fades.**

In the next chapter, we'll discuss another major advantage—how an IPO helps you eliminate debt and unlock massive financial leverage.

CHAPTER - 16

THE IPO WEALTH FORMULA - PAYING OFF DEBT & UNLOCKING EXPANSION

Why IPOs Are a Wealth Creation Tool, Not Just a Fundraiser

For many business owners, an IPO is seen as a way to raise capital. But the **real power of going public isn't just about getting cash—it's about financial leverage.** When done right, an IPO transforms your company from a profit-dependent business into a high-value, capital-efficient machine.

One of the biggest advantages of an IPO is the ability to **eliminate debt, restructure financial obligations, and unlock new growth opportunities.** Instead of relying on loans with high interest rates, you now have access to **public market funds that don't require repayment.** This financial freedom gives you a competitive edge, allowing you to reinvest strategically while strengthening your balance sheet.

How an IPO Helps You Wipe Out Debt

Debt is often a necessary tool for private companies, but it can also be a burden. An IPO provides a golden opportunity to **pay off**

liabilities and reduce financial strain. By allocating a portion of IPO proceeds toward debt repayment, businesses can eliminate costly interest payments and free up cash flow for expansion. Public companies also gain better financing terms, as banks and investors see them as lower-risk entities post-IPO.

Additionally, lowering debt improves your company's creditworthiness, which in turn allows for **better lending terms in the future.** A company with little to no debt has the financial flexibility to seize new opportunities without being weighed down by obligations to lenders. This puts public companies in a far stronger position to negotiate long-term growth strategies.

Beyond that, eliminating debt **increases shareholder confidence.** Investors prefer financially stable companies with a low debt-to-equity ratio because it reduces financial risk. A company with minimal debt has a stronger balance sheet, making it an attractive investment opportunity.

From Debt-Driven Growth to Capital-Fueled Expansion

Private businesses often rely on **debt-driven growth**, using bank loans or private equity funding to expand. This approach can be limiting because debt always comes with strings attached—interest payments, restrictive covenants, and lender control.

Post-IPO, companies transition to **capital-fueled expansion,** where their valuation and investor confidence drive financial strength. This shift allows businesses to make bold moves without worrying about debt burdens, ensuring long-term financial sustainability.

Moreover, investor-backed capital provides **greater operational agility.** Instead of being pressured to make short-term decisions to meet loan obligations, public companies can focus on **long-term wealth creation and sustainable business growth.**

Why Cash Flow Control Matters More Than Ever Post-IPO

Just because you raise millions (or even billions) doesn't mean you can spend recklessly. **Public investors expect responsible capital allocation.** Companies that mismanage funds post-IPO often face stock price declines and investor distrust. That's why managing cash flow wisely—balancing reinvestment with profitability—is critical.

The best-performing IPO companies follow a **disciplined financial strategy,** ensuring that their spending aligns with long-term business objectives. They also develop robust **investor relations programs** to maintain market confidence, ensuring continuous access to capital for future expansion.

Many successful companies reinvest IPO proceeds into **high-yield business areas** such as R&D, customer acquisition, and infrastructure development. These areas drive long-term value creation rather than just short-term revenue spikes.

Another key element of post-IPO financial strategy is **dividend management.** Some companies choose to reinvest all earnings into growth, while others distribute dividends to attract long-term investors. Understanding the right approach for your company's financial health is crucial to maintaining strong investor relations.

Mastering the IPO Wealth Formula

The key to long-term financial success post-IPO is strategic capital management. Companies that use their newfound financial leverage wisely will not only eliminate debt but also set the stage for continuous expansion.

IPO funds should not just be seen as an immediate cash influx but as **a war chest for sustained market leadership.** The companies that succeed post-IPO are those that **balance aggressive growth with financial discipline,** ensuring that every rupee raised is put to work in a way that generates long-term shareholder value.

An IPO isn't just about **raising money—it's about transforming your company's financial future.** Those who understand this formula will thrive, while those who misuse capital risk falling behind.

In the next chapter, we'll explore another major advantage—how an IPO helps you scale faster by leveraging automation and future-proofing your business.

CHAPTER - 17

SCALING SMART - HOW IPOS FUND AUTOMATION & FUTURE-PROOFING

Why Automation Becomes Essential Post-IPO

Once a company goes public, the pressure to **maintain performance, drive efficiency, and scale operations** increases significantly. Investors demand long-term growth, and that means companies can't afford to rely on manual, outdated processes. **This is where automation comes in.**

An IPO provides the capital required to **streamline workflows, optimize supply chains, and leverage technology** for operational efficiency. The businesses that use IPO proceeds wisely invest in automation to reduce costs, improve accuracy, and scale faster than their competition.

Automation also helps businesses avoid **bottlenecks** that often arise during rapid expansion. Many companies experience scaling issues post-IPO due to operational inefficiencies that were manageable when they were smaller. **By investing in automation early, businesses can prevent future challenges and ensure a smoother growth trajectory.**

Additionally, public companies face **higher compliance requirements** and **greater investor scrutiny**. Automation ensures that companies maintain regulatory standards efficiently without needing to scale their workforce disproportionately. The ability to generate real-time financial reports, maintain transaction transparency, and ensure compliance with market regulations becomes a **critical advantage** in sustaining post-IPO success.

How IPO Capital Powers Automation & Scalability

Smart companies allocate a portion of their IPO funds toward automation in critical areas such as:

- **Manufacturing & Production:** Automating assembly lines and production processes reduces labor costs, increases output, and improves quality control.

- **Supply Chain Management:** AI-driven logistics and predictive analytics help businesses optimize inventory and reduce wastage.

- **Customer Service & Sales:** Chatbots, AI-powered CRMs, and automated marketing campaigns enhance customer experience while reducing human resource costs.

- **Financial & Compliance Reporting:** Automating financial audits and compliance tracking reduces errors and ensures transparency for public investors.

- **HR & Talent Management:** AI-powered hiring tools and automated training programs streamline workforce expansion and talent retention.

- **Data Analytics & Decision-Making:** Implementing machine learning and AI-driven insights helps companies make data-backed strategic decisions faster.

√ **Risk Management & Fraud Detection:** AI-based systems analyze transaction patterns, detect fraudulent activity, and minimize security threats in financial operations.

The Competitive Edge of an Automated Business

The post-IPO phase is where companies either scale successfully or struggle to manage growth. Those that embrace automation **gain a significant competitive edge** by reducing dependency on manual processes and enhancing operational efficiency.

Companies that fail to implement automation often face **rising operational costs, inefficiencies, and scalability challenges**. In contrast, businesses that integrate smart technologies post-IPO are able to rapidly expand into new markets, increase profit margins, and maintain investor confidence.

Furthermore, automation enables businesses to **reduce operational risks**. Human errors, delays, and mismanagement are common challenges in fast-growing companies. By automating critical processes, businesses can mitigate these risks and **ensure consistent performance across departments**.

Another advantage of automation is its ability to **enhance customer retention and brand reputation**. Companies that automate their customer interactions—through AI-powered chat support, predictive behavior tracking, and personalized marketing—see greater customer satisfaction and loyalty. With increased investor expectations, maintaining strong brand equity through seamless customer experience becomes **non-negotiable** for post-IPO businesses.

Future-Proofing: Using IPO Capital to Build for Long-Term Success

Beyond immediate efficiency gains, automation also plays a critical role in **future-proofing** a company. Industries evolve, market demands shift, and businesses that fail to adapt get left behind. **IPO funds should be used to invest in emerging technologies that secure long-term success.**

Companies can future-proof themselves by:

- **Investing in AI and Machine Learning**: Businesses that leverage AI for analytics, product development, and customer insights position themselves for sustained market leadership.

- **Building Scalable Digital Infrastructure**: Cloud computing, cybersecurity, and automated data management systems ensure stability and scalability.

- **Developing Smart Manufacturing Capabilities**: IoT (Internet of Things) and robotics integration enhance efficiency in production and logistics.

- **Enhancing Cybersecurity Measures**: Public companies handle vast amounts of financial and customer data, making security a key priority for long-term sustainability.

- **Adapting to Changing Consumer Behavior**: Automated data tracking allows businesses to adjust their products, marketing, and services based on real-time consumer trends.

- **Leveraging Predictive Analytics**: Advanced data forecasting allows companies to anticipate market trends and customer demands, enabling them to pivot strategies efficiently.

- **Integrating Sustainable Business Practices**: Automation reduces environmental impact by optimizing resource usage, cutting waste, and improving energy efficiency.

The Smart Path to IPO-Driven Growth

Scaling after an IPO isn't just about expanding operations—it's about doing it **efficiently, strategically, and sustainably**. Companies that prioritize automation and future-proofing not only secure their position in the market but also **gain investor confidence, reduce risks, and maximize profitability.**

An IPO isn't just about raising funds—it's about using those funds **wisely** to build a business that stands the test of time. Companies that integrate **scalable automation strategies** ensure that their operations grow seamlessly, without hitting the common pitfalls of rapid expansion.

With this, we wrap up the core transformation that an IPO brings. The journey doesn't end at going public—it's just the beginning of **a new era of exponential growth, financial power, and market dominance.** The companies that thrive post-IPO are the ones that **think ahead, invest in technology, and execute a clear long-term vision.**

Those that fail to embrace automation and scalability risk stagnation and loss of investor confidence. The winners are the ones who use their IPO capital to build a company that not only grows but evolves and dominates its industry.

CHAPTER - 18

SHARES AS COLLATERAL – USING YOUR STOCK TO SECURE BUSINESS LOANS

One of the most **underrated weapons** of an IPO? **Your company's stock becomes a financial power tool.** The minute you go public, your shares aren't just numbers on a screen—they're **leverage.** Leverage for expansion. Leverage for funding. Leverage for taking the next big leap.

Private businesses struggle with securing loans. Banks demand assets, financials, and a laundry list of guarantees. But when you're public? **The game changes.**

Why Banks LOVE Public Companies

Banks see publicly traded companies as **safer bets** than private ones. Why? Because public companies have a **higher level of transparency**, are regulated by market forces, and have constant investor scrutiny. Unlike private businesses that operate in a financial black hole, public companies **must disclose their numbers every quarter**—which means banks have real-time data to evaluate their risk.

The result? **Public companies get loans easier, at better terms, and with fewer hurdles.**

Banks also offer **higher loan-to-value (LTV) ratios** for public companies, meaning you can borrow more money against your shares compared to a private company pledging hard assets. Instead of putting up your office building or machinery, you can simply **use your stock as collateral**—keeping your operations intact while securing growth capital.

Turning Shares into Borrowing Power

Using company shares as collateral means **you don't have to sell equity or take on high-interest loans** to get the capital you need. Instead, you pledge your stock to the bank, they hold it as security, and you get access to funds. Simple.

Why This is a Game-Changer:

- **Easier Loan Approvals:** Public companies get **faster approvals** because their stock provides liquid, high-value collateral.

- **Lower Interest Rates**: Secured loans always cost **less than unsecured ones.** Pledging shares reduces risk for the bank, so they give you better terms.

- **No Ownership Dilution**: Need money? You don't have to sell new shares or lose voting power. You keep control.

- **More Borrowing Power**: High stock valuation? That's more capital at your disposal.

- **Better Relationships with Banks**: Lenders prioritize **stable, growing, publicly listed companies** over private businesses with uncertain cash flow.

- **Emergency Liquidity**: If markets crash or funding dries up, you can **tap into your shares** instead of making desperate business moves.

Strategic Ways to Use Collateralized Shares

Smart companies don't just **pledge shares randomly**—they use them strategically to fund game-changing moves:

- **Expanding into new markets**: Instead of waiting for profits to accumulate, use pledged stock to **enter new territories NOW.**

- **Acquiring competitors**: Why spend years fighting for market share when you can **buy out your rival** and dominate overnight?

- **Launching new product lines**: R&D and marketing costs are high, but instead of taking high-interest loans, you can use your stock as an interest-free source of capital.

- **Funding infrastructure upgrades**: Need new offices, better technology, or streamlined production? Use your stock, get cash, and scale up without touching your bank balance.

Real-World Examples: How Giants Use Stock as Collateral

- **Reliance Industries** has used stock pledging multiple times to **fund massive expansion projects** without selling equity.

- **Adani Group** has effectively leveraged stock-backed loans to fund large-scale infrastructure projects across India.

- **Tata Group** has strategically pledged subsidiary company shares to secure funding without diluting its stakes.

If billionaires and conglomerates are **leveraging their shares for unlimited capital**, why wouldn't you?

The Dark Side: Risks & How to Avoid Them

Pledging shares comes with **serious risks** if not managed properly. The biggest one? **Margin calls.**

If your stock price **tanks**, banks can demand **additional collateral** or force you to **repay part of the loan immediately.** That's why you **NEVER over-pledge your shares.**

Risk-Proofing Your Share Pledges:

- **Don't Pledge Too Many Shares**: Keep your loan-to-stock ratio **conservative** so a market dip doesn't wipe you out.

- **Have Backup Liquidity**: Always have **cash reserves** in case banks demand additional collateral.

- **Use Loans for Growth, Not Survival**: Never pledge shares just to cover short-term cash flow gaps—it's **too risky.**

- **Monitor Stock Prices Closely**: If your stock is volatile, don't pledge shares that could trigger margin calls.

- **Diversify Your Financing**: Don't rely only on pledged shares; combine with **debt, equity, and retained earnings**.

The Future: How Stock-Backed Lending is Evolving

Financial institutions are **doubling down** on stock-backed lending because it's a win-win. Expect to see:

- **AI-driven lending decisions**: Banks will use real-time AI to offer **instant loans based on stock fluctuations**.

- **Crypto & Blockchain-backed stock loans**: Future lending models may combine **tokenized assets and traditional stock-backed loans** for greater flexibility.

- **New lending products**: Banks are developing **customized loans for high-growth public companies**, offering even better terms for those with strong market traction.

Final Takeaway: If You're Public, Use It to Your Advantage

Going public isn't just about **raising money once**—it's about creating an **ongoing financial powerhouse**. If your company has publicly traded shares, you're **sitting on a goldmine of capital.**

Don't make the mistake of **ignoring** this financial lever. The smartest companies use their stock **to fuel expansion, secure funding, and build long-term market dominance.**

The question isn't *"Should I use my stock for funding?"*—it's *"How soon can I start leveraging it to win the game?"*

CHAPTER - 19

SHARES AS CURRENCY - LIQUIDATING STOCK FOR BUSINESS GROWTH

Most founders think **raising capital means selling more shares, taking bank loans, or hunting down investors.** But the moment your company goes public, you unlock a financial tool that **private business owners can only dream of—your shares become currency.**

This is **one of the most powerful wealth-creation advantages** that an IPO gives you. Need money for expansion? Growth? Personal wealth-building? **You don't need a bank, a VC, or an investor's approval.** You already have an asset you can convert into cash—**your stock.**

Your Own Financial Reserve – Selling Shares for Immediate Cash Flow

Unlike private business owners who **struggle to extract value** from their company, public company founders have an **on-demand cash machine.**

If you need capital—whether for business expansion, a new acquisition, or to fund personal wealth—you can **liquidate a portion of your shares at any time.** And here's the kicker— you can do it **without diluting control** or being stuck with loan repayments.

Why This is a Game-Changer:

- **No More Funding Delays**: Need capital fast? **Selling shares takes days, not months.** No lengthy loan approvals. No VC meetings.

- **Use Funds Without Debt Burden**: Selling stock means **no repayments, no interest, and no pressure.**

- **Controlled Exit Strategy**: You don't have to **sell your entire company** to get liquidity. You can sell in small portions over time.

- **Enables Business Flexibility**: Liquidated shares can be **used for expansion, mergers, or even launching entirely new ventures**—without taking on debt.

- **Immediate Market Validation**: If investors are **buying your shares**, it's proof that the market believes in your company's future.

This ability to turn **your company's stock into real money on-demand** is what separates public company founders from private business owners who are **stuck waiting for buyouts, loans, or outside funding.**

How Founders & Promoters Use Stock to Fund New Ventures

Many of the world's biggest business leaders have **strategically liquidated their shares** to fund new projects, acquisitions, or entirely new businesses. They don't wait for investors to believe in their next big idea. **They fund it themselves.**

Real-World Examples:

- **Elon Musk** has sold Tesla shares multiple times to **finance SpaceX, The Boring Company, and even Twitter.**

- **Infosys Founders** liquidated stock over time to **diversify investments without losing company control.**

- **Vijay Shekhar Sharma (Paytm)** used equity liquidation to **reinvest into high-growth areas.**

- **Jeff Bezos** sold Amazon stock to finance **Blue Origin**, his space exploration company.

- **Mark Zuckerberg** has strategically sold Facebook (Meta) stock to **fund philanthropic initiatives and new business expansions.**

These founders **didn't wait for investors to back their ideas—** they used their **own equity as fuel for future success.**

Stock as an Acquisition Tool: Buying Companies Without Cash

Beyond liquidity, **shares can also be used as currency in acquisitions.** Instead of paying **hundreds of crores in cash** to acquire a competitor or startup, you can **offer shares instead.**

This is **how tech giants like Google, Amazon, and Facebook** have **acquired companies without draining cash reserves.**

Why This is a Massive Advantage:

- **Preserve Cash Flow**: Instead of wiping out cash reserves, you use shares as a trade.

- **Attract Founders & Executives**: Startups you acquire are more likely to sell to you if they get stock instead of just cash.

- **Align Interests**: If acquired companies take stock, they now have **a vested interest in your success.**

- **Flexible Deal Structuring**: Share-based acquisitions allow **negotiating better terms**, reducing upfront financial burden.

Institutional Investors & Stock Liquidity

When you're private, your business wealth is **locked in your company's valuation.** But once you go public, investors, mutual funds, and financial institutions are **ready to buy your stock at market prices**—giving you constant liquidity.

More trading volume = **easier access to cash without impacting stock stability.** High liquidity attracts **big investors, hedge funds, and institutional capital** that reinforce your company's market value over time.

This is why **being public is an ongoing advantage, not just a one-time event.**

The Hidden Risks of Selling Shares & How to Avoid Them

While selling shares is a **powerful funding tool, reckless selling** can create problems:

- **Stock Price Drops:** If founders **sell too many shares too quickly,** the market sees it as a **red flag.**
- **Investor Panic:** Large sell-offs can signal that leadership **doesn't believe in the company's future.**
- **Loss of Control:** Selling too much stock means **losing voting power.**
- **Tax Implications:** Liquidating shares triggers **capital gains taxes,** so planning is essential.

How to Sell Stock Without Damaging Market Confidence:

√ **Sell in Small Portions Over Time:** Avoid bulk selling that triggers investor panic.

√ **Time Your Sales Wisely:** Sell when the stock is strong, not during market dips.

√ **Publicly Announce Sale Reasons**: If you're selling to fund expansion or reinvest, **communicate it clearly.**

√ **Diversify Funding Sources**: Don't rely solely on selling shares—balance with **retained earnings, collateralized loans, and new fundraising rounds.**

The Future: How Companies Will Use Stock as Currency Even More

With global markets evolving, **expect stock-based transactions to become even more dominant.** Future trends include:

- **Crypto & Blockchain-backed Stock Liquidity**: Companies might tokenize shares for faster liquidity options.

- **AI-Driven Stock Trading for Business Funding**: AI models will **optimize stock sales** for liquidity without hurting valuation.

- **More Stock-for-Stock Mergers**: Instead of traditional buyouts, companies will **trade equity stakes as acquisition currency.**

Final Takeaway: If You're Public, You're Already Wealthier Than You Think

Most private business owners **wait for funding,** hoping for the right investor, bank, or buyer. Public company founders? **They create their own capital.**

Your stock is **more than just an investment vehicle**—it's a **financial weapon.**

You can fund new ventures, expand aggressively, buy competitors, or create generational wealth—all without begging banks or VCs for approval.

The question isn't "Can I use my shares for funding?" It's *"How fast can I start using them to build my empire?"*

PART 6:
FINAL WORDS –
MAKING YOUR MOVE

You've Seen the Blueprint. Now It's Time to Execute.

At this point, you know everything you need to take your company public, scale aggressively, and turn your IPO into a game-changing move. You've seen how businesses have leveraged the stock market to create **empires**, how founders used their public status to **expand, acquire, and dominate**, and why IPOs aren't just for the 'big guys'—they're for anyone with the **courage to think bigger.**

But here's the harsh truth: **Most business owners will never act.**

They'll sit on the sidelines, waiting for the "perfect time" to go public, waiting for their revenue to grow just a little more, waiting for some external validation. **And in that hesitation, they will lose.**

The difference between companies that scale to unimaginable heights and those that stagnate? **Action.**

History is filled with stories of businesses that **waited too long,** only to see their competitors take the leap and leave them behind. **If you don't move now, someone else will.**

The Fear of Taking the Leap

Every founder who has ever gone public has felt it: that **lingering doubt** that whispers, *What if I'm not ready? What if the market crashes? What if I lose control?*

This hesitation is natural. But **it's also dangerous**.

Think about the most successful companies today—Amazon, Tesla, Infosys, Reliance. Do you think their founders had **zero doubts** before making massive decisions? Of course not. They moved forward **despite the uncertainty**. They understood that **action is always better than inaction** because the cost of waiting is far greater than the cost of making a bold move.

The truth is, there will never be a "perfect" time to go public.

- Markets will always fluctuate.
- The economy will always have highs and lows.
- You will always feel like you need "just one more year" to prepare.

And yet, the companies that win **move anyway**.

Success Favors the Bold

No business empire was ever built by someone who played it safe.

The biggest, most transformative moves in business history have always been made by those who were willing to **bet on themselves**. Taking your company public is one of the boldest things you can do—not just for your business, but for your legacy.

- It sets you apart from your competitors.
- It gives you access to capital that private businesses simply don't have.
- It turns your company into an investment vehicle, not just a business.
- It forces you to level up your leadership, making you a **stronger, more strategic CEO**.

Companies that hesitate often **watch their competition go** public first—and by the time they decide to act, the market opportunity has shrunk.

The Missing Piece: Having the Right Partner in Your IPO Journey

You don't build a business alone, and you definitely don't take it public alone. Behind every successful IPO is a team that **knows the game inside out**—one that ensures everything, from valuation to market positioning, is done right.

If there's one thing that separates **seamless IPOs from chaotic ones**, it's the quality of the guidance behind them. Many companies make the mistake of trying to navigate the IPO process with a generic consulting firm or a fragmented team of advisors who focus only on compliance. **But the ones that truly dominate? They work with experts who see the big picture.**

The best IPO partners aren't just about **paperwork and approvals**—they help you:

- **Position your business for maximum valuation**, ensuring you're seen as an industry leader from day one.

- **Attract the right investors**, not just those looking for a quick flip but those who believe in your long-term potential.

- **Time your IPO perfectly**, taking advantage of market trends instead of reacting to them.

- **Develop a post-IPO strategy**, so your momentum doesn't stop at listing—it accelerates.

At this stage, you don't need just any advisor. **You need the right one.** And those who recognize this are the ones who go from simply "going public" to **dominating their market.**

What's Next? Your IPO Roadmap

If you've read this far, you already know you want to take action. Now, the only thing left is to **follow through**. In this final section, we're going to hammer home one last, crucial message:

- Why waiting too long to go public is the single biggest regret of most business owners.

- The real-life cautionary tales of businesses that hesitated—and lost big. ✓ Why the best time to act isn't **someday**—it's **right now**.

- A final **checklist** to get your IPO roadmap in place and make execution effortless.

- Bonus resources to help you become a high-level business leader, capable of not just running a company—but creating a lasting legacy.

It's Time to Make Your Move

The blueprint is in front of you. The opportunity is clear. Now, the only question left is: **Will you take it?**

You've done the thinking. You've seen the data. You've learned from companies that have made it big.

Now, it's time to **make your move.**

Exclusive Workshop: How IPOs Actually Work

CHAPTER - 20

THE BIGGEST REGRET OF MOST BUSINESS OWNERS – WAITING TOO LONG

The "Someday" Trap – Why Most Entrepreneurs Regret Not Going Public Sooner

Every entrepreneur tells themselves the same story at some point: *"Someday, I'll take my company public."*

They wait. For better revenue, better market conditions, better confidence. And in that waiting, they watch others make the move first. **By the time they're ready, the opportunity is gone.**

The biggest regret most business owners have? **Not acting sooner.**

It's not about whether they *eventually* went public. It's about the years they lost in between—the capital they couldn't access, the talent they couldn't attract, and the competitors who got ahead of them while they waited for the 'perfect moment.'

Here's the truth: **The perfect moment doesn't exist.** The companies that win are the ones that move **despite the uncertainty.**

Real Stories of Businesses That Hesitated… and Lost

Case Study 1: The Rise of Flipkart and the Fall of Those Who Waited

In the early 2000s, Indian e-commerce was **wide open**. Flipkart wasn't the first company to think of selling online—but it was the first to **scale aggressively** and seek investor backing when others hesitated.

While other startups debated whether India was 'ready' for e-commerce, Flipkart **raised billions, built infrastructure, and locked in customer loyalty.** By the time competitors like Snapdeal and ShopClues thought about taking the same approach, **Flipkart had already won the game.**

By 2018, Walmart acquired Flipkart for **$16 billion.** Many of its former competitors, once hesitant to scale, were either struggling or extinct.

The lesson? **You don't wait for the market to be ready—you make the market ready.**

Case Study 2: Paytm – A Cautionary Tale of Timing an IPO Wrong

Paytm, India's leading digital payments platform, was once seen as the future of fintech in the country. Founded in 2010, the company rapidly evolved from a mobile recharge platform into a comprehensive digital payments and financial services provider.

For years, Paytm was the undisputed leader in the digital payments space. But despite its strong growth, it hesitated on the IPO front. The company had originally considered going public earlier but delayed, waiting for 'better' conditions.

By the time Paytm finally launched its IPO in November 2021, the market was already shifting. Investor sentiment had changed, competition had intensified, and concerns over profitability had grown.

- The IPO aimed to raise ₹18,300 crore ($2.5 billion), making it India's largest-ever IPO at the time.

- Despite the hype, the IPO saw a lukewarm response, with only 48% subscription by the second day and barely scraping through full subscription by the final day.

- When Paytm debuted on the stock market, shares **plummeted by 27% on listing day**—a disastrous start.

- Over the next year, Paytm's stock lost more than **75% of its IPO value**, wiping out billions in investor wealth.

What went wrong? **Waiting too long.**

- Paytm's delay in going public meant that by the time it did, the market was flooded with competitors like Google Pay and PhonePe.

- Regulatory concerns over fintech companies had increased, making investors wary.

- Its IPO was aggressively priced, leading to concerns that the company was overvalued.

Had Paytm listed a few years earlier, **before market conditions changed and competition intensified, it could have secured a stronger market position and more favorable investor sentiment.**

The lesson? **Delaying an IPO in hopes of "perfect conditions" can backfire.** The market moves fast, and hesitation can turn an opportunity into a liability.**

The "What If" Regret That Kills Growth

Every business owner who hesitates eventually faces the same painful realization: *What if I had acted sooner?*

- What if I had secured funding before my competitors?
- What if I had expanded before the market got crowded?
- What if I had built a brand that investors trusted, instead of staying private for too long?

Entrepreneurs who take bold action don't have to ask themselves these questions. They don't live with regrets because they **moved when others hesitated.**

The difference between a **market leader** and a **company that fades into the background** often comes down to **who acted first**. And make no mistake—**the window of opportunity does not stay open forever.**

Why Right Now is the Best Time to Take Action

Every great entrepreneur understands one thing: **Timing is a myth.** The market will never be completely stable. The economy will always go through cycles. Your business will always feel like it could be *just a little more prepared.*

But the ones who make history **don't wait for the right time— they create it.**

Look at the biggest IPOs in India and around the world. Companies that went public during uncertain times—**Zomato, Nykaa, Paytm, Reliance, D-Mart**—they all faced challenges.

Yet, today, they are **market leaders.**

If you have a business that's growing, profitable, and scalable, then the question isn't *"Should I go public?"*

It's *"How much am I losing every single day I wait?"*

The Money Left on the Table by Waiting Too Long

Imagine you're running a profitable business. You're growing steadily. But instead of going public, you keep waiting, thinking you need another year or two to "perfect everything."

Here's what you lose:

- **Millions (or billions) in potential investment:** Private businesses rely on limited funding. A public company? It has **unlimited growth capital.**

- **First-mover advantage:** The first company to go public in an industry often gets the highest valuation. Every competitor who goes after you will look like a copycat.

- **Investor excitement:** The longer you wait, the harder it gets to excite investors about something truly new and fresh.

- **Your dream acquisition targets:** With IPO funds, you could **buy out** smaller competitors before they become threats. Without it? You're playing defense.

The cost of waiting isn't just **lost opportunity**—it's **the risk of being outpaced, outfunded, and forgotten.**

Final Checklist: Your Roadmap to IPO Success

Still hesitating? Here's your final checklist to ensure you're making the right move:

√ **Is your business generating consistent revenue?** If yes, public capital can help you scale faster.

√ **Are you competing against companies that are already public?** If yes, waiting only lets them strengthen their lead.

√ **Are you relying on debt or private funding?** If yes, an IPO can reduce dependency and increase your financial security.

√ **Is your industry experiencing growth?** If yes, public investors are more likely to back your expansion.

√ **Are you ready to build a legacy instead of just a business?** If yes, then the time to act is now.

The Time to Move is Now

At this stage, you already know that taking your company public is the next step. You've seen the case studies, the strategies, and the opportunities.

Now, there's only one thing left to do: **Execute.**

The longer you wait, the harder it becomes. **The opportunity is here, right now. The only question is—will you take it?**

Inaction is the greatest risk. Waiting is the greatest mistake.

The winners of tomorrow are making their moves **today.**

The only thing left to ask yourself is: **Will you be one of them?**

Get 1-on-1 IPO strategy advice on WhatsApp.

THE ULTIMATE GUIDE TO LONG-TERM BUSINESS & PERSONAL SUCCESS

Beyond the IPO – Building a Business and a Life That Lasts

Taking your company public is a huge milestone, but it's not the final destination. **The best entrepreneurs don't just build successful businesses; they build lasting legacies.**

A great IPO gives you access to capital, credibility, and growth opportunities—but what separates those who thrive long-term from those who fade into irrelevance?

The answer? **Continuous learning, strategic thinking, and personal evolution.**

This chapter is designed to be your **personal growth and business mastery roadmap**, packed with insights from the most powerful books on money, leadership, and scaling a business. These aren't just bestsellers; they are **must-reads** for every founder who wants to go from successful to legendary.

The Psychology of Money – Mastering Wealth & Financial Thinking

By Morgan Housel

Key Takeaway: *Being rich is about making money. Staying rich is about managing money wisely.*

This book is essential for entrepreneurs because it dives deep into **how successful people think about wealth, risk, and long-term financial decision-making**. The biggest mistake many founders make? **They assume capital will always be available.** But smart entrepreneurs understand that money is a tool to be **preserved, multiplied, and used strategically.**

- **Why you should read it:** It teaches you how to think about money in a way that ensures financial success, not just business success.

- **How it helps post-IPO:** It provides a framework to manage and reinvest capital wisely, rather than falling into the trap of reckless expansion.

The Lean Startup – Scaling with Precision & Speed

By Eric Ries

Key Takeaway: *Growth isn't about spending more money—it's about testing, adapting, and iterating faster than your competitors.*

Even after an IPO, companies that continue to operate with **lean, agile decision-making** are the ones that dominate. **Blind spending and overexpansion kill businesses.** The Lean Startup methodology helps founders build a **culture of innovation, rapid testing, and customer-centric decision-making.**

- **Why you should read it:** The IPO isn't the endgame—it's the start of the next phase. Scaling properly means continuously testing ideas and adjusting based on data.

- **How it helps post-IPO:** Ensures that you **stay adaptable** and don't fall into the trap of assuming all capital should be deployed immediately.

Good to Great – Becoming an Iconic Business

By Jim Collins

Key Takeaway: *The difference between good companies and great ones? They focus on their strengths, build elite teams, and maintain discipline.*

This book is an essential read for any founder looking to build an **enduring company that outperforms the competition for decades.** Collins' research shows that **great companies don't chase trends—they double down on their core strengths and execute with precision.**

- **Why you should read it:** It provides a framework for long-term success, even after you've achieved initial financial milestones.

- **How it helps post-IPO:** Helps founders avoid the **"IPO success trap"**—where companies relax after going public and lose their edge.

The Hard Thing About Hard Things – Real Leadership Lessons

By Ben Horowitz

Key Takeaway: *Running a business is messy. Every great entrepreneur faces brutal challenges—but those who survive know how to make tough decisions when it matters most.*

Many founders assume that once they raise capital, everything gets easier. **That's a lie.** The truth? More money means **more responsibility, more complexity, and more difficult choices.** This book is a raw, no-BS guide to handling **post-IPO leadership struggles, crises, and high-pressure decision-making.**

- **Why you should read it:** IPOs don't solve problems—they create new ones. This book prepares you to handle high-level challenges with confidence.

- **How it helps post-IPO:** Teaches founders how to **manage a growing team, handle investor pressure, and make the hard calls that keep a business thriving.**

Atomic Habits – The Science of Consistency & Success

By James Clear

Key Takeaway: *Success isn't about one massive breakthrough—it's about small, consistent actions that compound over time.*

Many entrepreneurs assume that their biggest achievements will come from **one single moment of brilliance.** But **true success comes from disciplined execution, daily habits, and continuously improving 1% at a time.**

- **Why you should read it:** It helps business owners build the personal habits that drive success, day after day.

- **How it helps post-IPO:** Ensures that even after going public, you stay **focused, disciplined, and in control of your time and priorities.**

Beyond Business – Building a Life of Wealth, Impact & Fulfillment

Going public will change your life. But it's important to remember that **your identity is bigger than your company.** Many founders make the mistake of thinking **their business is their entire existence**—and when challenges arise, they don't know how to handle them.

This is why long-term success isn't just about money—it's about purpose, balance, and legacy.

The Founder's Personal Development Blueprint:

1. **Master Money:** Read *The Psychology of Money* to build financial wisdom.

2. **Master Scaling:** Read *The Lean Startup* to scale with strategy.

3. **Master Leadership:** Read *Good to Great* to lead an exceptional team.

4. **Master Decision-Making:** Read *The Hard Thing About Hard Things* to handle pressure.

5. **Master Personal Discipline:** Read *Atomic Habits* to build consistency.

Success isn't about **how much money you raise**—it's about **how well you use it, how strategically you grow, and how intentionally you live.**

If you've come this far, you're not just building a company—you're building a legacy. **Now, it's time to make it unstoppable.**

Your Complete IPO Success Blueprint

PART 1: MINDSET SHIFT – THINK LIKE A MARKET LEADER

- Have you eliminated small-business thinking and embraced **scaling big**?
- Do you understand that **fear of losing control** is a myth, and IPOs can actually give you more power?
- Have you acknowledged that **staying private limits growth**, while IPOs unlock **unlimited capital** and credibility?
- Have you studied real-world case studies of businesses that **hesitated too long and lost**?
- Are you mentally prepared to **become a public company leader**?

PART 2: PRE-IPO PREPARATION – FIXING YOUR BUSINESS BEFORE GOING PUBLIC

- Have you **cleaned up your financials** to ensure they are **SEBI-compliant and investor-friendly**?
- Have you structured your company to avoid the **"family business trap"** (proper governance, external board members, and clear leadership roles)?
- Have you ensured your business is **scalable**, with a clear roadmap for future expansion?

- Have you identified your **competitive advantage**—why investors should choose you over competitors?
- Have you crafted your **IPO story** that excites and attracts investors?
- Have you conducted an **internal IPO readiness audit**?

PART 3: THE IPO PROCESS – STEP-BY-STEP EXECUTION

- Have you **selected a merchant banker** with a proven track record?
- Have you **conducted due diligence** to ensure no financial or legal issues arise during the IPO process?
- Have you **determined your IPO structure** (Fresh Issue, Offer for Sale, or Hybrid)?
- Have you correctly priced your IPO based on **market conditions, investor demand, and company valuation**?
- Have you prepared your **Draft Red Herring Prospectus (DRHP)** for SEBI approval?
- Have you planned an **investor roadshow** to generate demand before the IPO launch?
- Have you secured **SEBI approval** and set a launch date?
- Have you built a strategy for **IPO subscription and ensuring a successful listing day**?

PART 4: IPO VALUATION & INVESTOR ATTRACTION

- Have you used the **right valuation method** to ensure investors see your IPO as an attractive opportunity?
- Have you avoided the **3 biggest IPO pricing mistakes** (overvaluation, underpricing, or ignoring market conditions)?

www.ingramcontent.com/pod-product-compliance
Lightning Source LLC
LaVergne TN
LVHW041313200726
843509LV00009B/477